Times of Refreshing

The Rev. Dr Mark Stibbe gained a senior scholarship at
Trinity College Cambridge, where he studied English
and was awarded a double first.

After a spell teaching, he began training for the
ordained ministry in the Church of England, and
studied for a second degree in Theology at St John's
Nottingham. In 1989 he completed a PhD on John's
Gospel.

He is vicar of St Mark's Grenoside in Sheffield, and
Lecturer in the Department of Biblical Studies at the
University of Sheffield. A leading charismatic theologian, he is a popular writer and speaker at home and
abroad.

He is married to Alie and they have three children.

Other books by the same author

John as Storyteller (CUP)
A Kingdom of Priests (DLT)
John's Gospel (Routledge)
Explaining Baptism in the Holy Spirit (Sovereign World)

Times of refreshing

A practical theology of revival for today

DR MARK STIBBE

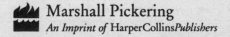
Marshall Pickering
An Imprint of HarperCollins*Publishers*

Marshall Pickering is an Imprint of
HarperCollins*Religious*
Part of HarperCollins*Publishers*
77–85 Fulham Palace Road, London W6 8JB

First published in Great Britain
in 1995 by Marshall Pickering

1   3   5   7   9   10   8   6   4   2

A catalogue record for this book is
available from the British Library

ISBN 0 551 02959–5

Typeset by Harper Phototypesetters Limited
Northampton, England
Printed and bound in Great Britain by
HarperCollinsManufacturing Glasgow

To Tim and Carol Fordham
loyal supporters and great friends

Acknowledgements

I would like to express my gratitude to one or two people who have helped me greatly in the writing of this book.

First of all I want to thank Christine Smith at HarperCollins for inviting me to undertake the project; secondly, various kind brothers and sisters in the Lord – such as Philip Smith, Paddy Mallon, Ken Gott, David and Mary Pytches, Sue Hope, Michael and Julia Mitton, Tim and Carol Fordham – who gave me plenty of good counsel along the way; thirdly, my wife Alie, and our three children (Philip, Hannah, Johnathan), who had to do without me for the five weeks it took for me to write this book; fourthly, to the people of St Mark's Grenoside, who gave their blessing to me spending so much time on this during December 1994, and who prayed hard for God's anointing upon it; finally, of course, to the Lord, for giving me the time, the energy, the motivation and the words. To him be the glory!

Contents

The Need for Biblical Theology

I often tell a story about an English vicar who hears about a big, successful church in the USA and decides to fly over and investigate. When he arrives he finds that the church building is situated amidst massive grounds, with sports hall, seminary and other modern facilities. As the senior pastor of the church shows him round, the vicar sees a large, spectacular building.

'What's that?' he asks.

'That? Oh, that's our science research block. That's where all the folk in our church who are scientists do their studies.'

'Can we have a quick look round?' asks the vicar.

'Why certainly,' his host replies.

The next minute they walk through the smart entrance hall, through the reception area, and into a main hall where men and women in white coats are busy at work. In front of him, the vicar sees a glass cabinet framed in wood. In the heart of the glass cabinet is a brain, perfectly preserved in various liquids.

'What on earth is that doing here?' the vicar asks.

'That's an Anglican brain,' the senior pastor replies. 'It's the perfectly preserved brain of an Anglican clergyman who was an expert on canon law, liturgy and faculties. It's very valuable indeed. In fact, it's worth $25,000'.

Expressing some surprise, the vicar walks on. A few minutes later he spies another cabinet with a perfectly preserved brain in it. This time the cabinet is framed in silver.

'What's this one?' he asks.

'That's a Methodist brain. It's the brain of a person who was an expert on the Wesley brothers, on Methodist hymnody, and on all matters relating to the Methodist Church. It too is very valuable. In fact, it's worth $50,000.'

A few moments later the two come across a third cabinet, also containing a brain, but this time framed in gold.

'What's this one?'

'This', replies the host, 'is our *pièce de résistance*. This is a Charismatic brain.'

'How much is that worth?' asks the vicar.

'$100,000.'

'Goodness me,' the vicar replies. 'Why is it worth so much more than the others?'

'Because it's mint condition – never used!'

Normally, when I tell that story, people laugh – the reason being, of course, that those of us who are Pentecostals or Charismatics have a reputation for being somewhat naïve theologically. That is fast changing as I shall explain in a moment. But I still find people coming up to me at conferences and asking, 'Why do you people always complicate things? Why do we need theology? Let's just get on with doing the works of Jesus and living in the power of the Spirit. Let's just live this stuff, not theologize about it.' No wonder Charismatics have a reputation for having two brains – one lost, and the other out looking for it!

The Holy Spirit and Theology

Behind questions like 'Why do we need theology?' there is however a quite legitimate concern – a concern about the nature and the role of theology in relation to the things of the Holy Spirit. Most Pentecostal and Charismatic Christians have a particular image of theologians and Bible scholars which is not altogether inaccurate. That image is of men and women who study the things of God using a purely rationalistic, scientific and cerebral methodology. Not surprisingly this kind of scholarship often ends up being irrelevant and cynical. It is perceived by many down-to-earth, committed Christians as a destructive product of the natural mind rather than as an anointed and worthwhile ministry. Part of the concern over doing theology in the context of the renewal is therefore a quite valid one. People want to know how on earth a discipline which is so influenced by the Enlightenment values of scepticism and rationalism can possibly help us understand the ways of the Spirit.

However, things have changed quite dramatically over the last ten years. Not all theologians are unbelieving radicals. In fact, there is right now a burgeoning movement of Pentecostal and Charismatic theology in the world. In an article entitled 'The Theology of Renewal and the Renewal of Theology', I recently pointed out that the Pentecostal churches are now producing a significant number of high-calibre theologians and Bible scholars. I showed how Pentecostal theology has, since the Second World War, gone through a number of distinct phases. In the first phase, Pentecostals who were academic did not feel free to write on overtly Pentecostal subjects. The scholarly environment was altogether too hostile to permit that. So these scholars separated their spirituality from their studies and wrote PhDs on aspects of the Bible and theology which were not directly or overtly related to Pentecostal spirituality. In the second phase, however, Pentecostals took a bold step forward and started writing historical and sociological studies of aspects of their church life and history. This second phase led to the third phase which we are in right now, in which Pentecostals are openly writing in an academic and Spirit-filled way on all sorts of subjects, from the spiritual gifts to Pentecostal spirituality.

Today Spirit-filled Christians (and that includes Charismatics as well as Pentecostals) are making a 'vital' contribution to theology and Biblical studies. There is now a Journal of Pentecostal Theology, which is supplemented by book-length studies on areas of interest to both Pentecostals and Charismatics. There is the centre portion of the magazine published by Anglicans for Renewal which is called *Skepsis* – a portion wholly devoted to the theology of renewal and the renewal of theology. There is a growing number of courses of interest to Spirit-filled academics in Great Britain alone. Last year I gave a course of lectures on 'The Holy Spirit in the New Testament' (subtitled 'Issues in Charismatic Theology') here at Sheffield University. Dr David Graham does something similar at Glasgow Bible College, as does Dr Max Turner at London Bible College. Everywhere there is evidence that the Holy Spirit is breathing new life into the arid wasteland of academic theology and Bible scholarship. Books, articles, courses and conferences are appearing all over the place – like green shoots in the desert.

This radical change in theology is therefore significant. It is a gift from God which provides both credibility and guidance for Spirit-filled believers.

The Renewal of Theology

What is different, then, about the way in which Pentecostals and Charismatics do their theology? Why should this kind of theology have any credibility amongst Pentecostal and Charismatic Christians? There are a number of key distinctions which I will outline briefly. For the sake of convenience I will refer to this genre of theology as the theology of renewal, TR for short.

The first thing about TR is that it is Biblical. Most Pentecostals and Charismatics revere the Word of God. Though an emphasis on experience of the Spirit can lead to a forgetfulness of the Scriptures in some circles, this is not the case right across the board. There are some modern-day Gnostics about in the Charismatic movement – people, in other words, who claim direct revelation from the Spirit and who bypass or ignore the written Word of God. But the vast majority of Pentecostals, Charismatics and renewed evangelicals believe that the Bible is the inspired and authoritative revelation of God's nature and God's acts. That is the *terminus ad quem*, the starting point, for all theological reflection in TR. At the heart of TR is a reverence for the Scriptures.

The second thing about TR is that it is experiential. It does not seek to negate all notions of the experience of God. Rather, TR is a reflection on real experiences of the Living God in space and time. TR therefore celebrates rather than denigrates the experience of God, particularly supernatural experience. In TR you will therefore find an attitude of openness rather than of suspicion when it comes to subjects like miracles, tongues, prophecy, dreams, worship, and so on. Furthermore, those who do TR will try to do so under the anointing of the Holy Spirit. They will seek the experience of inspiration as they study and write.

The third distinctive feature of TR is that it is devotional in character. No serious Pentecostal or Charismatic scholar conducts his or her studies as an isolated, intellectual exercise. Rather, such scholars do their work as an act of devotion or worship. Above their desks they inscribe the motto, *Hoc scrinium mea ara est*, 'This desk is my altar'. They subscribe to G. K. Chesterton's view that good theology is 'a worshipping of God with the mind'.

A fourth thing about TR is that it is communal in nature. All true Pentecostals and Charismatics are allergic to the individualism inherent in most academic study of the Bible and theology. Most university lecturers and professors study God, church history and the Scriptures in ivory towers, answerable to no one, and saying pretty well what they like. In TR, however, things are very different. Scholars involved in TR write mainly from within church communities. They are often supported both prayerfully and financially by such communities, and more often than not, much of their work grows out of teaching given within such communities. What is ultimately published is therefore a community product. It is the result of a group of believers reflecting on issues which they deem important to their everyday lives.

The final distinctive about TR is that it is practical. TR is not into irrelevant, highbrow games. All scholars involved in TR write on issues which arise out of practical experience. They also write in the hope that their work will result in actual, practical consequences. Theology, in TR, is therefore intimately connected with what is called *praxis*. It is seriously committed to the task of helping people to live out the liberating truth of God in the ongoing struggles of life.

A Practical Theology of Revival

These five distinctives are producing something of a renewal in the world of theology. They also lie at the heart of this present book, which is subtitled 'A practical theology of revival for today'. In the first place, every chapter has been constructed with reference to Scripture. Indeed, each chapter involves detailed exegesis of Bible passages. These are used to illuminate certain aspects of revival theology and practice.

In the second place, this book is experiential. In every chapter you will find narratives taken from the experience of both churches and individuals. All the narratives about churches are taken from well-documented historical sources. All the narratives about individuals are equally well-attested. They are from people I trust and respect. In every chapter, therefore, you will find narratives of experience – experiences which we will subject to theological reflection.

In the third place, this book is devotional. I have found that the thoughts which are communicated here have arisen out of contexts of worship. Some of them have come to me in the form of what I believe to be prophetic revelation. Others have come from hearing the Word of God being preached. In every case, they have arisen from a worshipping heart rather than a detached mind. They have evolved out of 'the head in the heart'.

In the fourth case, this book has proved to be a truly communal project. Many of its pages could not have been written at all had it not been for people giving me Bible passages which they deemed relevant to the present work of the Spirit. Certainly I have benefited greatly from having testimonies sent to me by friends. Most precious of all, I have had the opportunity to speak to some great saints of the renewal, such as Rev. Philip Smith, Bishop David Pytches, and others. This book therefore arises from community life. Indeed, my church has commissioned me to write it with the laying on of hands. Even as I write these words, some of the saints at St Mark's are praying for me.

Finally, this book is practical. This is a practical theology of revival. There are sections for further study at the end of the chapter. These can be used in group settings or on your own. The whole book is designed to help people caught up in the current 'revival' atmosphere to know how to respond and how to act.

The Need for Biblical Theology

Why have I written this book? There is a simple answer to this: because we need a practical theology of revival to guide us through these exciting days. As a result of the extraordinary events surrounding the Toronto Airport Vineyard Church (from January 1994 onwards), we now find ourselves with an urgent need for theological reflection on questions like, 'Is the Toronto blessing a revival? What does a revival look like anyway? Why is the experience of drunkenness in the Spirit so prevalent at the moment? What about extraordinary phenomena, such as ecstatic laughter? What do I need to do to receive at this time? What happens if I condemn the Toronto blessing?' If such questions are not addressed properly, I see real dangers ahead. The power of God without the Scriptures is a dangerous combination. We therefore need Biblical theology. The lessons of previous revivals are there for us all to learn. When church leaders stress the Spirit but neglect the Word, the work is discredited and diminished. As R. E. Davis tellingly puts it:

> At times of spiritual awakening there is a paramount need for sound teaching and instruction. When those who are revived are themselves taught in the truths of God's Word, they can properly interpret their own experience, adequately proclaim the truth to others, and also correctly instruct new converts. When this is not the case, or when they fail to properly instruct converts of the revival, there is a strong possibility that there will be dangerous extremes of belief and practice, and

that the whole movement of awakening and revival will not produce lasting fruit. In the case of the 1904 Welsh Revival, many believe that Evan Roberts' neglect of preaching and instruction was the cause of the awakening's failure to achieve its full potential.

That last point is worth emphasizing. R. B. Jones records what happened when Evan Roberts – the leading light in the Welsh Revival – became too exhausted to preach from the Word during revival meetings:

> Alas! under the terrific nervous strain of those days, the continuing of such teaching became to Mr Roberts a physical impossibility. And thus he could but sit silently in the pulpit, and take but little part other than in quiet prayer, a spectacle rather than a prophet.

Jones' judgement is that this was a turning point. He writes that 'the perspective, which the years that have followed supply, compels the judgement that this was a vital loss'. He explains why:

> The Word of God is not only pure but also purifying. Its giving forth, whether in reading, preaching, or teaching, has a vital effect on a meeting's atmosphere and success, for it lays an effectual check upon any elements therein that may be carnal.

The Lessons of Asuza Street

Previous revivals should alert us to the truth made popular in many sermons, that

> The Word without the Spirit, and you'll slow up.
> The Spirit without the Word, and you'll blow up.
> But Word and Spirit together, and you'll grow up.

The dangers of the spirit without the Word are particularly visible from the great revival centred upon 312 Asuza Street, Los Angeles, from 1906 onwards. God did many astonishing things amongst the first Pentecostals there. But reading the narratives of those involved in the leadership of that work reveals that the same neglect of Biblical theology which became true for the Welsh Revival in 1904 soon appeared in Los Angeles.

Frank Bartleman's book, *What Really Happened at Asuza Street?* – first published in 1925 – is particularly instructive in this respect. A number of things emerge from his account which may give a clue as to why the Asuza Street mission had terminated by 1911.

1 Sermons were not prepared at all. Bartleman himself declares, 'I never prepare what I shall speak.' Spontaneity rather than preparation was the key thing.

2 Series of sermons were therefore never considered. Bartleman writes: 'No subjects or sermons were announced ahead of time, and no special speakers for such an hour.'

3 No one was asked to preach in a meeting. Bartleman stresses that

The Lord was liable to burst through any one. We prayed for this continually. Some one would finally get up anointed for the message. All seemed to recognize this and gave way. It might be a child, or a woman, or a man. It might be from the back seat or the front. It made no difference.

4 Sometimes preaching was replaced by words given by the Spirit. Bartleman rejoices in one place that 'No attempt was made to preach. A few messages were given by the Spirit.'

5 Theologians were regarded with great suspicion.

6 The intellect was regarded as thoroughly polluted by sin.

Thus Bartleman criticizes one Pentecostal church for 'drifting toward intellectualism', and he describes the mind as a whole as 'the last fortress of man to yield'.

Some of these value statements may give an indication why the Asuza Street mission become torn apart through doctrinal division. The fact is, when the Word of God ceases to be central in the life of the church, that church becomes prey to all sorts of disasters. There is no doubt that the Pentecostal revival was in part a much-needed reaction against churches where doctrine had repressed experience and where reason had repressed emotion. It was certainly a timely corrective to a spirituality influenced by the rationalism of the Enlightenment. But the Word and the Spirit are supposed to go together. We are not to be ignorant of the Scriptures, nor are we to be ignorant of the power of God. We are to be fully cognizant of both. As Spurgeon said in his dying appeal, 'Men will not doubt God's Word when they feel His Spirit.' Where the Welsh revival went wrong, and Asuza Street too, was in its repudiation of sound and dynamic instruction from the Word of God. In their worship of spontaneity, and in their outright hatred for any hint of organisation, the leaders of these two revivals revealed the very same carnality which they strove so hard to avoid. That is a mistake which we cannot afford to make again.

Biblical Foundations

The reason I have written this book is therefore to provide some Biblical, theological foundations for what is, I feel sure, a history-changing work of the Spirit. In chapter 1 we will look at an historical overview of the major revival movements of the twentieth century. It is vital that the present generation of Spirit-filled believers should have a greater sense of what the philosopher Gadamer calls 'a historical consciousness'. Too much of our contemporary spirituality is profoundly existentialist in character. The experience of the present moment is all that matters. In chapter 1 we will look more closely at the 'former things'.

In chapter 2 we will look whether or not the Toronto blessing is a major movement of the Holy Spirit. We will also attempt to answer the question, 'What does a revival look like?' and then map the Toronto blessing against a list of chief characteristics.

In chapter 3 we will look at some of the cultural reasons why particular features – such as drunkenness in the Spirit – surface in times of revival. Here I want to propose that God adjusts his ministry to the needs of the hour. Since our postmodern culture is one which emphasizes experience, particularly bodily and ecstatic experiences, I will propose that the current wave of phenomena (particularly drunkenness in the Spirit) is God's way of getting the attention of a particular generation.

In chapter 4 we will look at the extraordinary phenomena which often attend major advances in the Kingdom of God. I will highlight the kinds of questions we should be asking, and then apply these to the recent phenomenon of ecstatic laughter.

In chapter 5 we will look at the spiritual preconditions for receiving from the Spirit in times of refreshing. Here I will try to sketch a charismatic theology of the desert experience. It seems to me that the most common preparation for refreshment is the admission of one's desperate thirst and utter dependence upon the Lord.

In the conclusion I will end with a couple of warnings arising from the disturbing concept of 'blasphemy against the Holy Spirit'.

Finally, in reading this book, please be aware that all theology is provisional not final. My comments are not the last word on any of the topics discussed. In many ways, each chapter is a discussion starter not the final viewpoint. My prayer is that you will exercise the gift of discernment as you read and that you will apply what is of the Holy Spirit and ignore what is not.

chapter one
Historical Background

* *

Strange things are happening in many churches today. As church leaders return from an unassuming building in Toronto called The Airport Vineyard, many of their churches are in turn being visited by the Holy Spirit in a profound and dramatic way. People are breaking into ecstatic laughter, falling down, crying, being healed, shaking, behaving as if drunk, and – most importantly – either getting converted or rededicating themselves to the Lord Jesus Christ.

In the midst of all of this, liquid imagery is abounding. There is much talk of a new 'wave' of God's blessing. There is also talk in Toronto of 'the backwash effect' – of getting drenched by the Spirit as you minister to someone else. I have seen people in times of ministry actually miming the effects of splashing water onto the person receiving prayer. Above all, people of all denominations are drawing attention to the striking vision in Ezekiel 47:1-12, where four waves of blessing flow one after another from the Temple, healing the land and renewing even the *Arabah* (the Depression). This present move of God, they argue, is one of these waves of the Spirit.

A Vision of Ezekiel

* * * * * * * * * * * * * * * * * * * *

In any work of renewal there are usually favourite passages of Scripture, passages which preachers regard as prophetic for the times in which we live. Twenty years ago it was Ezekiel 37:1-14, the vision of the valley of dry bones. The work of the Spirit, it was argued then, is a work involving the transformation of a dead church into a Spirit-filled army. Today, Ezekiel is back in fashion. This time, however, it is Ezekiel 47:1-12, the vision of the four miraculous effusions of water from under the threshold of the Temple. Today people are claiming that the Toronto blessing is either a new wave of the Spirit, or the first signs of a new wave. Here is a good example.

The following is a summary of a sermon from Mike Breen, the rector at St Thomas' Crookes in Sheffield. Mike begins:

> Ezekiel 47 pictures a river flowing from within the temple in Jerusalem. From there it flows eastwards past a grove of fruit trees eventually descending into the Jordan rift valley, filling up the Dead Sea basin.

As Mike studied this Scripture early in 1994, 'it seemed that the vision of the river provided a pattern of renewal which had a beginning, a middle and an end'. Phase 1 is the Temple (encountering God in sacrificial worship). Phase 2 is the trees (the call to a fruitful ministry of healing in the world). Phase 3 is the terminus (evangelism). For Mike, this spoke volumes concerning where he was at the time. As he reflected on the three phases he had identified, he saw that he was about to move to phase 3,

> Unconditional commitment to reaching the lost and seeing the spiritually dead brought to life.

For the rest of the sermon, Mike moved on from his own story to the larger story of renewal as a whole. He seems to equate the work of the Spirit in the late 70s and early 80s with phase 2 in Ezekiel 47:1-12, 'the trees'.

> The ministry of John Wimber, building on that of David Watson, brought to me the reality of God's sovereign power in the ministry of healing and casting out demons. What a fruitful time that was. We learned to pray for one another and many people were drawn to taste and see the goodness of God.

Now, however, renewal seems to be moving from the trees to the terminus (phase 3):

Where is renewal going next? We can only expect that the river will become deeper and even more fast-flowing as it seeks its destination. We will inevitably meet the Arabah in which the Dead Sea is found. It is mentioned in Ezekiel 47 and literally means the 'great depression'. That's where the river is heading – where we least expect to find life.

This is the real significance of the Toronto blessing. As Mike concludes:

This is what we are seeing in the so-called Toronto wave. The main elements of the wave may indicate where we are going. For instance, the joy may be the Lord strengthening his church for mission . . . The shaking may indicate that God is . . . shaking everything that can be shaken, so that what is unshakable – his kingdom – is revealed. The refreshment may tell us that God is calling us to receive his life-giving water and give it to those who live in a spiritual desert.

Pentecostal Interpretation

Before we proceed to a closer look at Ezekiel 47:1-12, some comments are needed at this stage about hermeneutics – about the rules for interpreting Scripture. In the example above, Mike Breen's approach is a far cry from the liberal way of interpreting the Bible. The liberal approach, generally speaking, involves a very sceptical view of the supernatural. Anything to do with experience of the Holy Spirit is regarded as intellectually dubious. This was brought home to me with particular poignancy when I advertised my course on 'The Holy Spirit in the New Testament' at Sheffield University. In the flier I wrote that my aim was to examine the experience of the Spirit in the life of Jesus, the life of the first Christians, and in the churches today. The reaction of at least two of my colleagues was, 'You can't say that! It's not scientific.' Well, I did say it. The course was the best attended third year option, and at the end of it the students asked if they could actually experience for themselves what I had been teaching. They subsequently spent an evening over at our church where they too experienced the supernatural reality of the Holy Spirit.

The liberal would frown at Mike Breen's exegesis of Ezekiel 47:1-12 arguing that it is basically subjective. The conservative would also frown at Mike's exegesis. By a conservative I mean the kind of evangelical who is brought up to believe that interpretation consists of discovering the original sense of a Biblical text and applying it to the present situation. This kind of person would find Mike Breen's sermon as unacceptable as the liberal does. The conservative would say, 'You can't do this with Scripture! You can't take a prophecy concerning Israel and apply it to the present situation like this. It's not allowed!' The reason he or she would react in this way is because conservatives, like liberals, believe that the meaning of a Biblical text is what the original author intended in his original historical setting. Since Ezekiel the prophet could not have intended his words to refer to the Toronto blessing, it is therefore completely misleading to claim otherwise.

Both liberals and conservatives, then, are allergic to the kind of interpretation which we have just looked at. Both would argue that interpretation is a matter of discovering the objective meaning of a text using the scientific methods associated with historical criticism. Both would agree that Mike Breen's kind of exegesis is extremely subjective, and indeed, to be fair, there is a danger of that. There is always a danger of eisegesis (of reading a meaning into the text) when exegesis (drawing the meaning out of a text) is the primary task. However, both liberals and conservatives need to understand that people affected by Pentecostal spirituality (and I include Charismatics like Mike Breen in this) have a different approach to hermeneutics, to Biblical interpretation. To the liberal and the conservative, the Pentecostal will justly ask, 'Where in the Bible does it say that interpretation merely consists of uncovering the original meaning of the author in the original situation?'

This is a very pertinent question. If one examines the ways in which the New Testament preachers and authors use the Old Testament, one thing becomes immediately clear: Neither are primarily interested in what the real author meant in his *Sitz im Leben* (life-setting). In fact, they show very little concern for that. They are fare more interested in what God is doing right now, and in finding Scriptures which illuminate that. In short, they are more concerned with what is called a THIS-IS-THAT approach to interpretation. They start with the THIS that God is doing in the Church, and they then find – under the guidance of the Holy Spirit – the THAT in the Scriptures which explains that work. Thus, in Acts 2:16, when Peter stands up just after the Holy Spirit has fallen on the 120 believers in Jerusalem, he explains the work of the Spirit in both himself and in his community by saying,

THIS is THAT which was spoken by the prophet Joel (Authorized Version).

Pentecostals contend that a THIS-IS-THAT approach to Scripture is not only the way in which the New Testament authors use the Old, but it is also the way in which we should interpret the Scriptures today. The primary task of exegesis involves us perceiving what the Father is doing right now amongst us (like Jesus in John 5:19) and then allowing the Holy Spirit to lead us to Bible texts which elucidate that work. Like the hermeneutics discussed by liberation theologians, the important thing is 'contextualized exegesis' – understanding our own communal story in the light of the overarching story of Scripture. Thus, Mike Breen begins with the THIS that God is doing in himself and in the community of the Spirit, and then is led to the THAT in Ezekiel 47:1-12 which illuminates this divine work.

Testing, Testing, Testing

Pentecostal hermeneutics is therefore prophetic in character. It results in 'prophetic preaching'. Indeed, we should note that Peter, when he gets up to deliver his sermon in Acts 2:14, is said to 'lift up his voice' (AV translation). The original Greek verb translated as 'lifted up his voice' is *apophtheggomai* which is normally used of the inspired utterance of a prophet. Peter's sermon, which involves a good deal of THIS-IS-THAT exegesis, is therefore prophetic preaching. If anyone uses a similar approach to Scripture today, the same rules apply to their interpretations as apply to prophecy in general. All prophecy must be tested by the community of faith, who together exercise the spiritual gift of 'distinguishing between spirits' (I Corinthians 12:10). If discernment is not encouraged, then subjective interpretations which are the product of a wayward and often manipulative imagination will go unchecked. The effects of that can be truly disastrous.

So what are the criteria for testing such interpretations? Since chapter 2 will be devoted to the whole business of discerning a true work of the Spirit I will make only a brief comment here. One of the most important tests is whether the same interpretation is offered by other people who have had no contact with each other. After all, according to Jesus,

> It is written that the testimony of two men is valid
> (John 8:17, NIV).

One of the key questions to ask when looking at a prophetic interpretation like Mike Breen's is, 'Is the same thing being said by others?'

The answer to that is yes, and here I need to offer a personal word of testimony. Earlier this year I was invited to speak at a weekend away for one of the congregations at St Thomas' Crookes. On the Sunday morning I spent two sessions offering a THIS-IS-THAT interpretation of Ezekiel 47:1-12. My approach included the suggestion that the Toronto blessing might be the first signs of a fourth and mighty wave of the Holy Spirit in the twentieth century. At the end of those two sessions, a number of folk came up to me to make the same comment: 'This is amazing! We had Mike Breen at St Thomas' a few weeks ago to preach two sermons prior to his arrival as our new rector. His evening sermon at 6.30pm was almost identical to what you have shared with us this morning. What's going on?!' To which I replied, 'What's going on is that two people may be hearing similar things from the Lord. What you need to do is to test and see.'

I therefore venture to suggest that there may be something of the Lord in a THIS-IS-THAT approach to Ezekiel 47:1-12. So let us look at the text itself.

Four Waves of Renewal

Before anything else, we must remember the historical background of Ezekiel as a whole. The Pentecostal approach to Scripture does not neglect the kinds of questions which are posed by historical critics. A purely spiritual form of interpretation would result at best in allegory and at worst in the kind of super-spiritual interpretations associated with the Gnostic heresies in the early Church. No, Pentecostal interpreters and expositors regard the following subjects as extremely important: the original author's intention (such as it can be discerned), the original meaning of the passage (arrived at through the well-tested methods of historical criticism) and the original social setting of the passage. The reason why such questions are vital is because oftentimes a prophetic sense of THIS-IS-THAT comes as the Spirit-filled interpreter discovers a surprising accord between the situation of the Biblical author and the present situation of his community. Pentecostals therefore do not dismiss issues of history. Far from it.

So who was Ezekiel? Ezekiel was a priest who ministered in the Temple in Jerusalem. He was taken captive in 597 BC when the armies of Nebuchadnezzar, king of Babylon, captured Jerusalem after a brief siege. With the young king Jehoiachin and 'all the princes, and all the mighty men of valour, ten thousand captives, and all the craftsmen and the smiths' (according to 2 Kings 24:14), Ezekiel was taken from the Temple, which was his whole life, and then resettled in Babylon – in a little house in a dusty valley near to the river Chebar. In the fifth year of his exile (about 593 BC), he received a call from the Lord to a prophetic ministry to the house of Israel. He was about 30 years old at the time.

In exile, Ezekiel seems to have had relative freedom to come and go as he pleased. However, in his spirit he felt far from free. As a priest, he must have missed the Temple terribly. The homesickness and the sense of loss must have been unbearable. However, in the fifth year of his exile, Ezekiel had an amazing vision of the *merkabah*, the chariot-throne of Yahweh, which confirmed to him that the God of Jerusalem was alive, active and in control, even in the polytheistic land of Babylon. From then on, Ezekiel had a series of visions – including a vision of the rebuilding of God's Temple, the glory of Yahweh returning to the holy place, and renewal flowing out of that new Temple.

It is this promise of renewal which is so beautifully captured in Ezekiel 47:1-12. Out of the Temple in Ezekiel's vision (a future, restored Temple) flow four waves. The first is ankle-deep, the second knee-deep, the third waist-high, and the fourth too deep and dangerous to cross. These four waves are clearly symbolic not literal. As one commentator puts it, 'No amount of water-divining will confirm Ezekiel 47!' What then do these four waves symbolize? They symbolize movements and outpourings of the Holy Spirit. Indeed, we may recall John 7:37f, words uttered by Jesus (significantly enough in the Temple) at the Feast of Tabernacles:

> On the last and greatest day of the Feast, Jesus stood and said in a loud voice, 'If anyone is thirsty, let him come to me and drink. Whoever believes in me, as the Scripture has said, streams of living water will flow from within him.' By this he meant the Spirit . . .

There is a good deal of uncertainty about the correct interpretation of this verse. Did Jesus mean that streams of living water would flow from himself? Or did he mean that it would flow from the believer? Whichever interpretation is correct, one thing is certain. In John's theology, the Holy Spirit is given by the Lord Jesus Christ, and this Spirit starts to be given to the world from the Cross, where Jesus – lifted up, in the rich sense in which John uses that phrase – gives up his spirit (John 19:30). It is there, in that elevated place, that a stream of water flows miraculously from within his stricken body (John 19:34-5). Jesus Christ is therefore the new Temple. He himself implies as much when he says, 'Destroy this temple and I will raise it up again in three days.' John explains, 'The temple he had spoken of was his body' (John 2:19-22). The body of Jesus on the Cross is consequently a new temple, and the water flowing from the side of Jesus is the river of life which pours from the place of sacrifice. It is the stream of life-giving Spirit prophesied by Ezekiel in his magnificent vision. It is therefore the Lord Jesus, the Great Baptizer in the Holy Spirit, who is the reality to which Ezekiel's symbols point. It is he who must take centre stage as we reflect on the gracious outpouring of blessing prophesied in Ezekiel 47:1-12.

This is That

When I first studied Ezekiel 47 three years ago, I was struck by a sense of THIS is THAT (Acts 2:16). At the time, I think it was the number four which attracted my attention. Ezekiel has a fondness for that particular number: it occurs 40 times in the book. As early as Ezekiel 1:5 we are introduced to four living creatures. There are four main visions of Ezekiel as a whole. Four seems to be a key number. Why? Because in Ezekiel's time it was a number which symbolized totality or completeness. Hence Ezekiel 37:9: 'Come from the four winds, O breath!' i.e. come from every corner of the earth.

What struck me then and strikes me now is the fact that Ezekiel sees four waves of renewal, and that the fourth is clearly the one that completes the process. The early church fathers saw significance in that too. They perceived a pattern here in the way God's Spirit operates – a pattern for renewal, if you will. Some of them saw the four main missionary movements of the Spirit anticipated in Ezekiel 47: first Jerusalem, then Judea, then Samaria, and finally the whole earth (Acts 1:8). Others saw Ezekiel 47 as prophetic of the writing of the four gospels, with John's gospel being the most complete (the most 'spiritual') of them all. In diverse and creative ways, the fathers saw the THIS which the Spirit had richly produced in the first century in terms of the THAT which is foreseen by the prophet Ezekiel.

I would like to propose in this first chapter the following thesis: that in the twentieth century, we can speak of four main movements of God's Holy Spirit, and that these four 'waves' represent a THIS which corresponds to the THAT which we find in Ezekiel 47:1-12. Now there are obviously a couple of large claims within this thesis. First of all, there is the claim that we can speak of four waves of the Spirit in the history of the Church during this century. This claim seems to me to be historically sound. Pentecostal theologians and historians have recently been arguing that we have witnessed three distinct waves of the Holy Spirit thus far – three unplanned, divine movements of the Holy Spirit for the renewal of God's Church. In the *Dictionary of Pentecostal and Charismatic Movements,* these three waves have been identified as:

1 The emergence of Pentecostalism, arising from Asuza street in 1906;

2 The emergence of Charismatic Renewal in the early 1960s;

3 The emergence of Protestant Evangelical Renewal in the early 1980s.

I shall argue a little later that there is a fourth wave coming, and that the Toronto phenomenon is the first sign of it.

The second claim within my main thesis is the claim that the THIS which we see in the history of the twentieth century can be illumined in the light of the THAT which we read in Ezekiel 47:1-12. This is a harder claim to sustain on intellectual and academic grounds. In matters such as these we enter the realm of the prophetic, and academic scholarship has a poor track record when it comes to understanding and uttering prophecy. The main justification for regarding Ezekiel's vision as prophetic for our own context is that it depicts a pattern of renewal involving four stages. Whether this is the way the Holy Spirit always works is hard to say. The ways of the Spirit are mysterious; they are like the desert wind in ancient Palestine (John 3:8). At the very least, however, we can speak of a pattern of renewal portrayed in the Ezekiel text, a pattern involving four mighty and miraculous effusions of the Spirit from the heart of the Divine Presence. That, as we will now see, is a symbolic picture of what I believe has been happening (and indeed *is* happening) in the twentieth century.

Wave 1: Pentecostalism

In Ezekiel 47:3, the prophet is led by his mysterious guide through water that is ankle-deep. This water derives from the Temple, which has miraculously become the source of an efflux of divine, supernatural blessing.

I would like to propose that the Pentecostal movement (which began in the first decade of this century) can be likened to this initial, foot-washing wave of the Spirit. The Pentecostal movement has, after all, been described as 'the First wave' by Pentecostal and Charismatic theologians. It is a highly significant movement which is now widely recognized. Indeed, Lesslie Newbigin has called Pentecostalism the third great force in Christianity today (alongside Protestantism and Roman Catholicism). Steven Land, rather more fairly, has refined this thought as follows:

> Along with Roman Catholicism, Eastern Orthodoxy and Protestantism it [Pentecostalism] may be regarded as a 'fourth force' (as opposed to the usual 'third force' designation) in Christianity.

The origins of the Pentecostal movement go back as far as 1741, but the date usually given for the full appearance of this wave is 1906. The place where the wave broke was 312 Asuza Street, and the effects were dramatic. People were baptized in the Holy Spirit, given the gift of glossolalia, released into exuberant praise, propelled onto the mission field, and many other wonderful things besides. As William Seymour (the pastor of the church) joyously reported:

> The power of God now has this city agitated as never before. Pentecost has surely come and with it the Bible evidences are following, many are being converted and sanctified and filled

with the Holy Ghost, speaking in tongues as they did on the day of Pentecost. The scenes that are daily enacted in the building on Asuza Street and at missions and churches in other parts of the city are beyond description . . .

So, the heady days of Acts were restored. The Golden Age of the earliest Church had returned. Indeed, David Barrett writes this of Pentecostalism: 'the major characteristic is a rediscovery of . . . the supernatural with a powerful and energizing ministry of the Holy Spirit in the realm of the miraculous . . . This is interpreted as a rediscovery of the spiritual gifts of New Testament times, and their restoration to ordinary Christian life and ministry'.

The major distinctives of Pentecostalism appeared fairly quickly. We can identify the following as significant:

1 An emphasis upon 'baptism' in the Holy Spirit as a second blessing, subsequent to conversion (hence the term 'theology of subsequence'), in which the believer receives the Holy Spirit. This second blessing is regarded as 'power for service' or, more specifically, 'power for mission' (Acts 1:8).

2 The proof that this Spirit-baptism has been experienced is regarded as glossolalia, speaking in tongues. Tongues speech is quickly revered as 'Initial Evidence'. Though some Pentecostal denominations have made adjustments here (as indeed William Seymour did), glossolalia to this day remains a major distinctive of Pentecostalism.

3 The movement at Asuza Street was a movement amongst the marginalized. Asuza Street was typically described by the press as a 'tumble-down shack' with a 'coloured congregation'. Seymour himself wrote of this building as follows:

The meetings are held in an old Methodist church that had been converted in part into a tenement house leaving a large, unplastered, barn-like room on the ground floor . . .

In this ramshackle context, it was not surprising that Seymour's church attracted the poor and the marginalized. This was a meeting hall 'in the vicinity of tombstone shops, stables and a lumber yard' (Seymour's words). Like the stable in Bethlehem, it was a most unlikely place for heavenly visitations. Yet here the poor and the forgotten found a spiritual home. As Seymour later wrote:

> If it had started in a fine church, poor coloured people and Spanish people would not have got it, but praise God it started here. God Almighty says he will pour out his Spirit on all flesh . . . It is noticeable how free all nationalities feel.

So this was a church which broke down walls of racial and social prejudice. William Seymour was himself a sight-impaired black preacher who created a 'colour-blind' congregation where blacks, whites, Asians, Hispanics and others met regularly. Here the 'colour-line' was washed away by the blood of Christ. Though many later Pentecostals experienced 'redemption and lift' (i.e. upward social mobility), this emphasis on the poor is a major distinctive of Pentecostalism to this day.

4 Asuza Street became a launch-pad for bold missionary endeavours. Indeed, a passion for seeing the Kingdom extended in even the darkest parts of the globe became a common feature. Some of those given the gift of tongues assumed that this was the xenolalia of Acts 2:1-13 (i.e. the supernatural ability to speak unlearnt foreign languages) and went out onto foreign mission fields relying on this gift to get by! This teaching, promulgated mainly by Charles Parham, was quickly rejected!

5 Right from the start, Pentecostalism has been characterized by a reappearance of the more spectacular charismata of I Corinthians 12:1-11, particularly the gifts of healing, but also prophecy, knowledge and miraculous works. This, it should be noted, is something largely new in the history of revivals. There had been wide-scale revivals prior to Asuza Street, but recent studies have shown that the evidence does not suggest that these revivals involved a restoration of spiritual gifts. In his historical and theological study of revivals, R. E. Davis says this

about the appearance of spiritual gifts:

> The evidence of previous centuries is that usually they do not;
> the evidence of this present century is that quite often, but by
> no means always, they do (p. 231).

Indeed we may note the words of the eighteenth century theologian of revival, Jonathan Edwards: 'I do not expect a restoration of these spiritual gifts . . . nor do I desire it.'

6 Another feature of Pentecostalism was and is the spontaneity, exuberance and noisiness of its praise. Local newspapers in Los Angeles spoke of the 'howlings of the worshippers'! Lively music, passionate (largely unprepared) sermons, dancing, ecstatic utterances, all played their part in creating this effect. In particular, this was worship which involved the body – hands raised or clapping, or clasping on to God for a blessing, bodies swaying in the heavenly breeze. The whole body responded to this wave of blessing. The whole of the worshipping community was involved as well. There was no clericalism (priests only) here. Maximum participation was actively encouraged at every level of the church's life.

7 Eschatological fervour was another distinctive. Peter Hocken has recently written that 'Pentecostal-Charismatic Christianity is generally characterized by heightened expectation of the return of the Lord.' We may put this partly down to the reappearance of the charismata in the twentieth century. The Elim Pentecostals stated in 1932 that:

> The supernatural graces so indispensable at the beginning
> have become so once again because it is the end.

Eschatological fervour was a common feature. As the newspaper *Apostolic Faith* put it:

> 'Jesus is coming soon', is the message that the Holy Ghost is
> speaking today through nearly everyone that receives the
> baptism with the Holy Ghost.

8 A final important distinctive has been the stress upon narrative. Testimonies (personal stories of faith) abound in Pentecostalism. Particularly in the early days, oral story-telling was a common feature. Though the movement spawned the *Apostolic Faith* newspaper and a number of important, popular books, the emphasis (as one would expect in such a social milieu) was upon orality rather than textuality. The orality of liturgy and the narrativity of witness were constant characteristics.

All in all, the first wave of the Spirit this century was immensely significant and indeed effective. Today Pentecostals can be found in over 200 countries. There are tremendous numbers in East Asia, with renewal going on in Korea and China at an incredible pace. In 1988 there were 178 million Pentecostals world-wide. Right now the numbers are likely to be far larger. Indeed, David Barrett estimated that there were 205 million denominational Pentecostals in 1992.

So this first wave was indeed a massive, supernatural work of the Spirit. It was an 'ankle-deep' river of blessing. It may be that some significance may be drawn from this, for this wave washed the feet of those whom the historic churches were by and large not touching. This first wave was a foot-washing wave. Here the *me 'opsayim* ('water of ankles') of Ezekiel 47:3 washed the feet of the outcast, the impoverished and the marginalized. No wonder William Seymour described the Asuza Street phenomenon as, 'a mighty wave of salvation among the unconverted'.

Wave 2: The Charismatic Movement

In Ezekiel 47:4a, the guide leads Ezekiel through a second river of blessing, one which is this time knee-deep. The second wave, added to the first wave, raises the level and the momentum of the river from the Temple and out into the land beyond. It is into this water that the prophet now wades.

It is not without significance that there has been a second wave of the Holy Spirit in the twentieth century – the Charismatic movement which began in the early sixties. Few people are aware that there is a difference between Pentecostals and Charismatics, but the differences do exist and they are important. So what are they? In brief, Charismatics are Christians who have experienced many of the distinctives of Pentecostalism yet have remained, by and large, within their older mainline non-Pentecostal denominations. In the vast majority of cases, Charismatics are neo-Pentecostals who have, unlike their Pentecostal counterparts, decided to stay in their churches rather than go – though we should note that these Christians have been joined since 1965 by thousands of other independent Charismatic churches. These independents, since 1970, account for about 14% of the movement.

The history of the Charismatic movement is difficult to summarize. For a more detailed analysis, you need to read Peter Hocken's book entitled (significantly) *Streams of Renewal*. But a key moment seems to have been when Smith Wigglesworth gave a prophecy to a young Pentecostal pastor called David du Plessis:

> There is a revival coming that at present the world knows nothing about. It will come through the churches. It will come in a fresh way . . . It will eclipse anything that has been known in history. Empty churches, empty cathedrals, will be packed again with worshippers. Buildings will not be able to accommodate the multitudes.

The important thing about this prophecy is the mention of churches and cathedrals, for it demonstrates that the new wave which Wigglesworth anticipated was going to bless the historic churches. From this moment on, du Plessis became committed to a vision of sharing the Pentecostal blessings with the historic churches. Indeed, du Plessis became widely revered, especially through his work in the World Council of Churches, where he was known affectionately as 'Mr Pentecost'.

All this paved the way for the Second Wave. Du Plessis – with his openness to Christians in the mainstream traditional denominations – helped Anglicans, Catholics and members of other churches to become more open to what was going on in the Pentecostal movement. Indeed, the crown of his achievements was the development of Pentecostal-Catholic dialogue – one of the many good things which was made possible by Vatican II.

With this kind of groundwork, it was not long before Donald Gee was speaking of a 'new Pentecost', a new movement of the Spirit starting to become visible in the late fifties. This movement involved the occurrence of distinctively Pentecostal blessings (especially Baptism in the Spirit) but outside Pentecostal denominations and within the historic churches. The best-selling book *Nine O'Clock in the Morning* relates the story of Dennis Bennett (an Episcopalian priest who had a major influence in the 1960s, particularly on Anglican clergy). His story shows very powerfully how God intended this second wave for people within the mainstream denominations.

What this means is that the distinctive of the Charismatic movement are much the same as those which I identified for Pentecostalism, except that the context is different. Peter Hocken identifies the following distinctives of Charismatic renewal:

1 Focus on Jesus. Baptism in the Holy Spirit is seen as an encounter with the Lord Jesus. 'Jesus is Lord' is the common proclamation. It is the ascended Lord who baptizes in the Holy Spirit.

2 Heartfelt Praise. The first result of this Spirit-baptism is an overflow of praise from within the believer. A new capacity to glorify God is discovered. Spontaneity is the key.

3 Love of Scripture. Charismatics are typically Bible-carriers.

4 Divine Revelation. There is a conviction that God speaks today, not just through the Word but through the Spirit – particularly through the gifts of revelation. People who are baptized in the Spirit start to hear the Lord!

5 Natural Evangelism. Baptism in the Holy Spirit produces a compulsion to share Jesus and a naturalness in doing it. There is a new capacity to speak freely of the Lord to the unchurched.

6 Spiritual Warfare. There is a new awareness of the reality of Satan and the powers of evil. Deliverance therefore becomes a normal part of the church's ministry.

7 Spiritual Gifts. I Corinthians 12:8-10: the gifts in that text become normative, particularly tongues, healing and prophecy.

8 Eschatological Fervour. There is a heightened longing for the parousia.

Much of these (if not all) characterize Pentecostalism (the First Wave). However, there are three major differences between the first and second waves:

1 The churches in which the Charismatic renewal occurred were, by and large, the historic churches. The story of Dennis Bennett suggests this, as does the emergence of Charismatic renewal in the Roman Catholic Church (beginning at Duquesne University in 1967).

2 The kinds of people who were touched by CR (Charismatic renewal) were different. CR made its greatest progress in the white, middle-class sector of First-World societies. An interesting side effect of this has been a greater emphasis on inner healing rather than physical healing. This can partly be attributed to the greater awareness of modern psychology in middle-class milieux.

3 The attitude towards other denominations in CR – particularly the ability to form *koinonia* with members of other churches – distinguishes it from Pentecostalism. There is a greater ecumenism about CR, especially where there is a perceived fellowship in the Spirit which obliterates denominational boundaries.

As far as numbers are concerned, in 1988, Barrett estimated that there were 123 million charismatics worldwide. This second wave, combined with the first wave, has indeed produced waters that are knee-deep! If we are wondering just how, we should note Barrett's comment that 'Charismatics outnumber Pentecostals in numbers of annual converts worldwide'.

Wave 3: Protestant Evangelical Renewal

In Ezekiel 47:4b, a third wave emerges from the Temple. This wave, added to the previous two, produces a river which is waist-high. The river is getting deeper!

Here again we can draw parallels with the work of the Holy Spirit in the twentieth century, for Peter Wagner has identified a Third Wave of the Spirit. Indeed, he coined the term 'Third Wave' to describe a movement which is similar to Pentecostalism (First Wave) and to CR (Second Wave) yet which has some fairly important differences from both. This movement of the Spirit emerged in the early 1980s and a key figure is John Wimber. He was launched by God into a dramatic signs and wonders ministry in the late 1970s and his ministry has had a profound effect on millions of Christians worldwide.

Wagner defines third wave Christians as 'mainly evangelicals who have recently become filled with the Spirit, and who are experiencing the Spirit's supernatural and miraculous ministry. They emphasize signs and wonders and exercise gifts of the Spirit. These evangelicals have stayed within their mainline nonpentecostal denominations. They do not identify themselves as either Pentecostals or charismatics'. David Barrett agrees with this definition, and argues that the third wave is 'a major new revitalizing force'.

Wagner writes that 'The desire of those in the Third Wave is to experience the power of the Holy Spirit in healing the sick, casting out demons, receiving prophecies, and participating in other Charismatic-type manifestations without disturbing the current philosophy of ministry governing their congregations'. He defines the five chief distinctives of this movement as follows:

1 The belief that baptism in the Holy Spirit occurs at conversion, not as a second blessing. Release of the Spirit or 'possessing one's possessions' are the commonest phrases.

2 The expectation of multiple fillings of the Spirit subsequent to conversion (Ephesians 5:18), some of which may closely resemble what Pentecostals and Charismatics call baptism in the Holy Spirit.

3 A low-key acceptance of tongues as one amongst many charismatic gifts. A gift which is given to some but not to all, and a gift which is regarded not as initial evidence but as a prayer gift.

4 The ministry of healing. This rather than baptism in the Holy Spirit is the sign of initiation into Third Wave Christianity. The ministry of healing is most commonly corporate rather than individual. This is associated with signs and wonders. Phrases like 'power encounter' are frequently used.

5 A desire to avoid divisiveness at almost any cost. Compromise over raising hands in worship, public tongues, methods of prayer for the sick, is accepted in order to preserve unity of the body. The implication of second-class Christianity is strenuously avoided.

To this list we may add two other significant features. Both of these were shared with me by Rev. Philip Smith, a key figure in the CR in Britain in the sixties. When he first encountered the Third Wave, he was struck by two things:

6 Waiting on the Holy Spirit. Philip was pleasantly surprised by the way in which the minister encouraged a time of silence after the prayer, 'Come, Holy Spirit'. Times of reverent and expectant silence had not been a feature of his experience of Pentecostal or Charismatic meetings.

7 The Place of the Body. Though the ministry time might be led by someone from the front, what was remarkable to Philip was the role of that person. The person was acting as a charismatic facilitator – encouraging the gifts of the Spirit to be used in the body. This was not like Pentecostal meetings, or meetings he had experienced in CR, where everything tended to revolve around a sole figure, such as the Pentecostal evangelist. Here words of knowledge and pictures of a revelatory nature were being shared from the body during times of waiting.

In 1988, David Barrett estimated that there were about 20 million Christians worldwide who could be counted as Third Wavers. Now the figure is likely to be much larger. Barrett projects 65 million by the year 2000AD.

If we add this Third Wave to the streams of the First and Second Waves, we have an accumulative river of blessing that is waist-deep! Taken together, these Three Waves of the Spirit amount to a profound and dramatic work of God. Christians who would identify with one of these waves are found in 11,000 Pentecostal denominations and in 3000 independent Charismatic denominations, as well as 150 traditional non-Pentecostal ecclesiastical denominations. They are found in 8000 ethnolinguistic cultures, speaking 7000 different languages (not counting 'tongues'!), covering 95% of the world's entire population. By 1992, Barrett estimated that these Christians numbered 420 million (i.e. 24.5% of the world's Christians). Of these,

29% = white,
71% = non-white;

66% = Third World,
32% = Western;

87% = poor,
13% = affluent.

Furthermore, we are still seeing rapid growth in these three existing waves. As Barrett writes: 'All three waves are still continuing to surge in. Massive expansion and growth continue at a current rate of 19 million new members per year or over 54,000 per day – of which ⅓ is purely demographic (births minus deaths): ⅔ are converts.' By 2000AD, the projected figure is 562.5 million.

Wave 4: Global Revival

According to Ezekiel, there is a fourth wave coming. In 47:5, we read: 'He measured off another thousand cubits, but now it was a river that I could not cross, because the water had risen and was deep enough to swim in – a river that no-one could cross.' Clearly, the fourth wave in Ezekiel's vision is the wave which completes the process of divinely ordained renewal. It is one signifying completion and totality. It is a wave which, added to the previous three, produces a river which is both too deep and too dangerous to cross.

Looking at twentieth-century church history, it is hard to discern a fourth wave as such. So, is there a fourth wave coming? Are the present manifestations of the Spirit in Toronto and in many other places the 'sea-fret' of this fourth wave – the first splashes on our faces of a tidal wave of power which is about to break upon us? Only time will tell, but I do find it interesting that Smith Wigglesworth, who prophesied the coming of the Second Wave to David du Plessis, also prophesied the coming of a mighty work of the Spirit. One week before he died, he foresaw two great movements of God, one stressing the gifts of the Spirit and the other stressing the Word of God. When these two movements combined, Wigglesworth said that we would see the greatest movement of God's Spirit ever witnessed in church history.

Many today are picking up on his prophecy (Wigglesworth was right, after all, in his prophecy about CR). For me its importance and its accuracy are evident. In the post-war years (Smith Wigglesworth died in 1947), we have seen a movement emphasizing the gifts (CR) and a movement emphasizing the Word (Billy Graham, John Stott, F. F. Bruce, et.al.). The Third Wave, it seems to me, is a movement of God in which the Holy Spirit has been at work particularly amongst evangelicals, and this has resulted in the beginnings of that marriage of Word and Spirit predicted by Smith Wigglesworth. If this Third Wave is all about the reintegration of the Word and the Spirit, then that is significant. Smith Wigglesworth prophesied that it would be when Scripture and the Spirit – the two hands of God, according to Irenaeus – were united in one spirituality that the world would witness a huge revival. My deep conviction is that the current blessings witnessed in Toronto and in thousands of churches throughout the world are the first hints of a fourth wave.

If a fourth wave does break, what will be distinctive about it? Let me identify eight things, very tentatively, using Ezekiel 47:1-12. Using these verses as our guide, I suggest that we may see the following:

I. Great Sacrifice

Notice in verses 1-2 how the waves all flow from the area where the brazen altar of sacrifice is situated. They start from the southern corner of the Temple and flow past the altar of burnt-offering and then out of the eastern gate. This suggests to me that the fourth wave will involve sacrifice. That has been true of the previous three waves. Indeed, David Barrett has written of churches affected by the first three waves that

> Members are more harassed, persecuted, suffering, and martyred than perhaps any other Christian tradition in recent history.

The fourth wave, then, will cost us a great deal. It will be particularly from a global New Age religion (hostile to the idea of exclusivism) that this persecution and harassment will, I believe, derive. A new world order is beginning to emerge, and that new world order will embrace a New Age religion as part of its 'sacred canopy'. This religious system (already evident just about everywhere in the West, and increasingly in the East) will be profoundly pluralistic. In other words, it will stand on the belief that all religions are one; no one religion is all. In a global context where that kind of value becomes part of the political and social belief-structure, things will not be easy for Christians, or indeed I suspect for Jews. There will be a cost involved in being a Christian in the future. But where the sacrifice is greatest, there the harvest will be the richest and most plentiful.

2. Profound Spirituality

The fourth wave will produce a movement of depth. Notice how the waters become too deep and dangerous to cross once the fourth stream issues forth from the Temple (v. 5). This is deep water. There is nothing superficial here. This suggests to me that the fourth wave will not be cosmetic. It will not be manageable by any human, theological technology. It will be a profound, dangerous, enormous and elusive movement of God.

So there will be a depth to this Spirit-filled spirituality which we have not seen thus far. Where will this depth come from? Notice how the rivers of life in Ezekiel 47 issue from the Temple. This suggests to me that there is something singularly important about the Jewish roots of our faith. It suggests to me that it is in Judaism that the depth for this new wave of the Spirit will derive. Charismatic Christians are more and more looking for a sense of depth in their spirituality. Many recognize that we have bought into one of the characteristics of our age: superficiality. We have fallen for the modernist notion that only the new, the modern is worthwhile. However, there is now a reaction against this in Spirit-filled churches. Many Charismatics are going back to roots, studying Celtic Christianity and, further back, the Jewish roots of our faith. Many are rediscovering what Gadamer calls a 'historical consciousness'. The worship of the present moment is increasingly seen for what it really is – a dangerous, existentialist idolatry. Depth spirituality is what many of us are after, and depth will be a key characteristic of the Spirit's work as we approach the millennium.

3. Biblical Integration

There are trees on each side of the river produced by the fourth wave (v. 7). This reminds me of Psalm 1, and the tree planted by streams of water which symbolizes the person who meditates faithfully on God's Word. The trees in Ezekiel 47:7 are therefore a symbol of a people who are not forgetful of the Word. Frequently revivals have died out because of a lack of sound, Biblical teaching. The fourth wave, however, will be a movement in which the gift of teaching (the supernatural ability to provide dynamic instruction from Scripture) will be greatly evident. We may recall at this point that Jerome saw the river in Ezekiel 47:7 as an image of the teaching of the church: 'It flows along between two rows of trees, the books of the Old and the New Testaments, fructifies everything and even renews the Dead Sea of the souls which died in sin.' Clearly Biblical teaching is going to be essential.

However, we should note that the model of teaching will be different from the liberal and conservative approaches I mentioned earlier. Charismatics and Pentecostals treat Scripture differently from conservative evangelicals. In *Word and Spirit at Play*, Jean-Jacques Suurmond describes how Pentecostals approach and interpret Scripture:

> Scripture then is not treated as a legal code but expounded with the aid of a charismatic exegesis which resembles that of the prophets, the New Testament writers and rabbinic midrash. This includes a playful interaction between the text of the Bible and the present situation, in which the story of Scripture is interwoven with that of the community. Conversely, the believers recognize themselves in the text.

It is in this sense that there will be an integration of Bible and experience, Word and Spirit. A charismatic hermeneutic will emerge which will greatly facilitate the whole process of Biblical integration.

4. Supernatural Signs

In verse 8 the prophet observes the fourth wave cascading into the land beyond the desert, out into the eastern region, into the Arabah (the Depression) and entering the Dead Sea. 'When it empties into the sea', says the prophet, 'the water there becomes fresh.' The prophet witnesses, in other words, a great miracle – the desalination of the Dead Sea.

If this verse has anything to say about the fourth wave it is surely this: that we will see astonishing supernatural signs as this wave hits us. Signs and wonders described in previous revivals (like the Great Awakening) will be witnessed in reality. The level of *dunamis* (power) will increase, as will the level of *exousia* (authority). There will be greater power to heal the sick, deliver the oppressed, and to work wonders. There will be greater authority in the preaching and sharing of the Gospel. People will flock to churches which have been drenched by this Fourth Wave to *see* and to *hear*. Even the land will be affected by this wave. Even places that resemble the Depression will have an atmosphere of blessing and holiness (as in the Welsh Revival). Places that feel like the Dead Sea will lose that sense of bitterness which they have possessed for centuries.

Communities will be healed. The land will be saved.

So the fourth wave will involve a tremendous upsurge in *dunamis* which in turn will produce an equally awesome upsurge in *dunameis* (mighty works). Indeed, we will find it hard to assess some of the things we see against existing theological maps and grids. There will be a sovereign strangeness about much that occurs. Perhaps that is something which we are already beginning to witness. As the Spirit moves in power, particularly in churches affected by Toronto, there is a strangeness about a good deal of the supernatural phenomena being experienced. Indeed, several months ago I received a paper from the Vineyard Church in the USA entitled, 'What in the World is Happening to Us? A Biblical Perspective on Renewal'. This paper begins:

> Our purpose in putting this paper together is to develop a Biblical apologetic for what we see happening among us. Much of what we are seeing is strange to the natural mind. The following are some of the phenomena that we have seen in our meetings.
>
> 1. Falling
> 2. Shaking
> 3. 'Drunkenness'
> 4. Crying
> 5. Laughter
> 6. Prophetic revelation.

Already there is a mystery about the supernatural signs being witnessed. Perhaps these signs are just the foretaste of things to come.

5. Massive Growth

In verse 9 we are told that 'swarms of living creatures' will be visible wherever this river flows. 'There will be large numbers of fish' . . . As the river of the Spirit moves out into the land beyond the Temple, the commission to become 'fishers of men' will be realized in unimaginable ways.

Two things should be noted here. First of all, it is immediately clear that all four waves of the Spirit are not blessings which are confined to God's house. These are not movements which confine the blessing to the holy place! As Zimmerli points out in his commentary: 'the water, which is empowered in the innermost sanctum by the abundance of holiness on the part of the most holy one, flows out from the sanctuary into the dried up, salty region of mysterious curses . . .' There will therefore be an emphatically outer-directed quality about the fourth wave. Here is Zimmerli again: 'the decisive statement that blessing goes out from the place of the divine presence into the surrounding land cannot fail to be heard.' For those Pentecostal and Charismatic churches which have not emphasized sufficiently that the power is for evangelism not for entertainment, this is a timely though disturbing reminder.

Secondly, we need to take great encouragement from the word 'swarms'. This word suggests huge numbers of fish caught in the net of the Gospel. This will be a movement in which millions of souls find salvation in Jesus Christ. Instead of being jealous or suspicious of numbers, we will learn to rejoice in numbers. We will celebrate swarms of converts. The fourth wave will bring in an unprecedented catch. Indeed, where the fourth wave is affecting the life of local churches, we will be like the fishermen in verse 10 who stand along the shore, waiting for a daily, abundant catch of new Christians!

6. Extraordinary Variety

In verse 10, we are told that 'the fish will be of many kinds – like the fish of the Great Sea'. There will be a surprising and exhilarating variety about the people converted. We will rub shoulders with Messianic Jews, with the downtrodden and persecuted peoples of the base communities, with Eastern Orthodox Christians, with born again Gypsies and so on. We will be surprised by the kinds of people with whom we will share *koinonia* in the Spirit. I suspect that we will find a strange sense of oneness with people whom we would previously have written off. I believe that we will be surprised and excited by the kinds of people caught up in the fourth wave. Old prejudices will be broken down. Leaders who have avoided one another or hurt one another will be reconciled. Walls of division will be knocked over by the powerful force and momentum of this great wave of God.

7. Practical Compassion

In verse 12 we see the river vivifying fruit trees on both sides of the river. These trees will bear fruit every month and their fruit will serve for two things: healing and food. This shows that the fourth wave will be a movement which heals the sick and feeds the hungry. There will be no separation of evangelism and social action here. The fourth wave will be a wave which moves us to minister to the poor, to the oppressed, to the hungry. It will be a movement which not only restores the spiritual gift of teaching but also the spiritual gift of mercy (the two missing gifts in many contemporary, Spirit-filled churches). Indeed, in this wave, we will even minister healing and life in the Arabah: the Great Depression. We will recapture something of the foot-washing humility of our Pentecostal brothers and sisters at Asuza Street.

8. Divine Judgement

In verse 11, however, there is a word of warning. 'But the swamps and marshes will not become fresh; they will be left for salt.' What are the swamps and marshes? These are the churches which have become bogged down. They may be churches which have become bogged down in rigid, formal, lifeless traditions. They may also be churches which have been renewed but which have become bogged down in their own version of 'lifeless tradition'. They are most likely to be churches where the leadership exercise a doctrinal control over congregations – where the doctrine in question is hostile to the experience of the Holy Spirit in power today. So this verse contains a frightening warning.

DO YOU SEE THIS?

'Perhaps,' I hear you say. All this will need to be tested. However, the question posed in verse 6 to Ezekiel seems to me to be relevant for us also, 'Son of Man, do you see this?' Like Peter Hocken (in his recent book on the outpourings of the Spirit in the twentieth century, *The Glory and the Shame*), I do believe we have witnessed great things this century, but that these movements need to be seen and perceived. Above all, I believe, we need to see that there is a fourth wave coming. This wave – it seems to me – will be something quite glorious. Zimmerli reminds us in his commentary that the number four is 'the number of comprehensive totality'. The fourth wave of the Spirit, whose first signs we may be witnessing, may very well turn out to complete a process of renewal begun in 1904-6 with the Welsh Revival and the Asuza Street mission. Every new work of God requires spiritual perception on the part of the church. As Isaiah proclaimed,

> See, I am doing a new thing;
>> Now it springs up; *do you not perceive it?*
>>> I am making a way in the desert
>>>> and streams in the wasteland (Isaiah 43:19 NIV).

Or, as Bartleman put it in a tract in 1906,

> Opportunity once passed, is lost forever. There is a time when the tide is sweeping by our door. We may then plunge in and be carried to glorious blessing, success and victory. To stand shivering on the bank, timid, or paralyzed with stupor, at such a time, is to miss all, and most miserably fail, both for time and for eternity. Oh, our responsibility! The mighty tide of God's grace and favour is even now sweeping by us, in its prayer-directed course. There is a river (of salvation) the streams whereof make glad the city of God – Psalm 46:4. It is time to 'get together' and plunge in, individually and collectively . . .

chapter two
Exercising Discernment

• •

A few years ago there was a story circulating about a diocesan bishop in the Church of England. The bishop in question found himself taking a good many confirmation services at a time when there were different orders of service, such as series 2 and series 3. Having done a confirmation service one Sunday, he went the next Sunday to a nearby parish and began the service as he had the previous week.

'The Lord is here,' he declared.

There was no response. Thinking that the people could not hear, he said even louder:

'The Lord is here.' Still there was no response. A third time he said the words, this time shouting:

'THE LORD IS HERE!'

Still no response. So he turned to the vicar of the church and said:

'The Lord is here, isn't he?'

To which the vicar replied:

'Not in Series 3, he's not!'

That story is relevant to the subject I want to tackle in this chapter, a subject which can be cast in the form of two basic questions – the first to do with discernment, the second to do with definition.

1 How do we know if a movement such as the Toronto blessing is one initiated, directed and sustained by the Holy Spirit? In other words, how do we know that the Lord is here?

2 If we decide that something like the Toronto blessing is 'the Lord', how do we know what to call it? Should we call it a revival? Or should we call it a 'renewal', or an 'awakening', or what? How, in short, do we discern and define large-scale movements of God's Holy Spirit?

The Gift of Discernment
. . . .

When Paul wrote his first letter to the church in Corinth, there was a good deal of division in the fellowship there. There were many problems, including issues to do with sexual morality and resurrection theology, but the main bone of contention seems to have been the abuse of the more spectacular charismatic gifts – particularly *glossolalia*. Evidently there was a group of Christians who spoke in tongues, who were also particularly graced with the revelatory gifts, but who prided themselves on being a kind of spiritual elite in the church. The problems which this attitude produced are hinted at throughout chapters 12-14 of I Corinthians, where Paul addresses the need to exercise wisdom in the presence of ecstatic phenomena, the need for love and sensitivity on the part of all Christians where such gifts are manifested, and the need to maintain a sense of seemly order in charismatic assemblies.

In the midst of all this advice, perhaps the most important 'word of wisdom' is Paul's reminder that there are some people in every community of faith who are especially endowed with discernment. I am referring to verse 10 of I Corinthians 12 where, in a list of the spiritual gifts, Paul alludes to the gift of 'distinguishing between spirits'. The original wording in the New Testament Greek is, *diakriseis pneumaton*. The word *diakrisis* is a combination of *krisis* (judgement) and *dia* (through). *Diakrisis* is therefore the ability to 'see though' various things. It is the ability to pass a sure verdict on a particular phenomenon or behaviour. The word *pneumaton* is the genitive plural of the word *pneuma* which means 'spirit'. What is the meaning of *pneumata* in this context? We might think that Paul means spiritual gifts, especially given the overall topic of these chapters. But if that were so, he would have used either *pneumatika*, as he does in verse 1 of I Corinthians 12:1, or *charismata*. Here, however, he uses *pneumata* – spirits. What does this mean?

The consensus of those who have written on the gift of discernment is that *pneumata* in this context means the invisible spirits, energies or forces which work to influence us. These can be reduced to three fundamental categories: the *pneuma* of God, which is usually referred to as *hagios*, as the 'Holy Spirit'; the *pneuma* which is the spiritual part of our humanity, the 'spirit' with which we act and speak; the spirits, finally, which are unclean, unholy and supernatural in character (often called 'demons'), and whose purpose is destruction, deception and death. In brief, these three spirits are the Holy Spirit, our human spirit, and unholy spirits. With this in mind we should define *diakrisis pneumaton* as the ability to pass judgement on the different kinds of spirits which motivate behaviour and words. Paul is speaking about a special ability to discern whether the Holy Spirit, our human spirit, or an unholy spirit is influencing a particular *phanerosis* or manifestation (I Corinthians 12:7) within the ecclesial context.

As with all the other gifts mentioned in I Corinthians 12, this ability is a charism. The word charism comes from the Greek word *charisma* (plural = *charismata*), which literally means 'grace-gift'. In other words, all of the gifts listed by Paul are abilities generously lavished upon us as a result of the saving work of Jesus on the Cross. Saying that should not lead us into seeing these gifts purely as supernatural endowments. That would lead to the very dualism of supernatural and natural which led to the Corinthian problem in the first place! My own conviction is that the grace-gifts are, by and large, natural abilities which are redeemed, sanctified and energized by the Holy Spirit when we become Christians. Thus, people with a natural ability to communicate often find that they start to excel in the grace gift of teaching (Romans 12:7; I Corinthians 12:28). Others who have a naturally intuitive temperament often find that they start to receive visions, pictures and impressions from the Lord. Others who have an innate, natural leaning towards healing find that they are used to minister wholeness in Christ's name to the sick. In every instance, God turns natural abilities into spiritual gifts . . . by his grace.

This, I propose, is especially true of the gift known in common parlance as 'discernment'. There are naturally discerning people in the world – people whose own sense of refined intuition, common sense, training and experience make them adept at evaluating what lies behind people's words and actions. Such folk, once they are 'in Christ', will very likely find this natural gift is developed into a supernatural ability. Like all the other gifts, this discerning faculty is not something which is given to everyone in the Body of Christ. But it is given to some. It is not more important than all the other gifts. But neither is it less important. It is an ability which needs to be recognized by church leaders, and then used in the congregation. Indeed, many a shipwreck (both individual and corporate) would be avoided if those who are genuinely gifted in this area were properly recognized and used in the church. The body needs a nose as well as ears (I Corinthians 12:14-26). It needs people gifted at discerning evil as well as people gifted at hearing God.

Developing a Sense of Smell

As it was in first-century Corinth, so it is in twentieth-century Britain. In other words, both the Corinthian context and our own are characterized by religious pluralism and the quest for spiritual experience. Many different religions and mystery cults were on offer to both the traveller and the native in Corinth. At least some of the Corinthian Christians had been involved in ecstatic religious practices before they were converted. This much is implied at the start of I Corinthians 12, where Paul says, 'You know that when you were pagans, somehow or other you were influenced and led astray to mute idols.' Now however they had become new creations in Christ Jesus. They were therefore to be far more discerning about *pneumatika*, 'spiritual phenomena' (I Corinthians 12:1). In the great profusion of spiritualities in Corinth, the followers of Jesus were only to pursue those things which exalted Jesus Christ as Lord and which exhibited the great Christian virtue of love. In a cultural atmosphere pervaded by all kinds of different *pneumata* or spirits, the Corinthian church was only to welcome that which derived from the Holy Spirit.

Today we also live in a culture defined by religious pluralism. There are all manner of cults, pagan religions, New Age spiritualities and occult practices which compete with the Gospel. Indeed, one of the main characteristics of our so-called postmodern age is its promotion of a kind of pick 'n' mix mentality which actively encourages people to select and create their own spirituality. For example, yesterday I received the first edition of a magazine subtitled 'Sheffield's Guide to Positive Change'. On the inside cover there was an advert for Acupuncture and Chinese Herbalism. Page 2 invited me to join an organization known as Gnosis. Page 10 publicized a course on Tai-Ching and Qigong. Page 13 encouraged attendance at a Rebirthing Group devoted to experiencing the healing power of my breath. Page 15 had an advert for Reiki healing, page 17 for selfheal therapy, page 20 for life dancing, page 24 for meditation classes, and so on. In a culture like this, where actual experience of the spiritual realm is encouraged, and where a confusing myriad of spiritual practices vie for attention in the religious marketplace, people are prey to all kinds of harmful *pneumata*. Without a set of usable and legitimate criteria for testing spirits, people are very vulnerable.

The Importance of Discernment

It seems from the evidence that the author of I Corinthians was himself a man who often ministered in the gift of discernment. In Acts 16:16 Luke reports an incident which occurred when he was with Paul on one of their missionary journeys:

> Once when we were going to the place of prayer, we were met by a slave girl who had a spirit by which she predicted the future. She earned a great deal of money for her owners by fortune-telling. This girl followed the rest of us, shouting, 'These men are servants of the Most High God, who are

telling you the way to be saved.' She kept this up for many days. Finally, Paul became so troubled that he turned round and said to the spirit, 'In the name of Jesus Christ I command you to come out of her!' At that moment the spirit left her.

This incident is especially instructive for a number of reasons. First of all, it seems likely that the slave-girl actually possessed a spiritual ability to predict the future. She had what we might today call a genuine, psychic gift. Secondly, it is equally likely that this gift had proved accurate on a significant number of occasions. This woman's predictions, in other words, came true. Thirdly, she actually declared the truth when she shouted, 'These men are servants of the Most High God, who are telling you the way to be saved.' She was not telling lies. She was proclaiming the truth about Paul's mission. Fourthly, in spite of all these things, Paul eventually became extremely troubled by her behaviour. He saw through her words to the 'spirit' (*pneuma*) which lay behind them. That spirit the narrator identifies in Acts 16:16 as a *pneuma* by which the slave girl foretold the future. Fifthly, as a result, Paul said to the *pneuma* at work within her words which constitute a command to leave, in the name of Jesus Christ. Notice, Paul did not rebuke the woman but the spirit at work within the woman. He did not expel the person but the demon at work in the person. No witch-hunt here.

The reason why this story is so important is because it shows how essential it is to operate in the grace-gift of discernment. Some spirits, after all, produce what on the surface looks like plausible, acceptable and even authoritative behaviour. Some demonically-inspired behaviour even looks Christian. But not everything which sounds plausible and looks powerful is necessarily godly in origin. Not everything spectacular is necessarily sanctified. Witness the following example taken from a letter written by Firmilian to Cyprian in AD 256:

About twenty-two years ago . . . suddenly there arose here a certain woman who in a state of ecstasy put herself forward

as a prophetess and acted as if she were filled with the Holy
Spirit. But, on the contrary, she was being carried by the force
of the chief demons in such a way that for a long time she
disturbed and deceived the church, bringing about certain
astonishing and extraordinary things.

Suddenly one of the exorcists confronted her, a man who had
been proven and who always lived a religiously disciplined life . . .
rose up to subdue that evil spirit, which also had a short time
earlier, with subtle deceit, predicted that a certain opposing and
unbelieving assailant would come. However, the exorcist inspired
by the grace of God resisted strongly and showed that spirit
which was previously thought to be holy to be very evil
(Firmilian, *Epistulae Cypriani*, 75:10; R. Kydd's trans.).

It is possible that Firmilian's account is biased, but let us
assume for a moment that it is a fair representation of an actual
series of events – even given the gap of twenty-two years. What
is interesting again is the fact that the woman – like the slave-
girl in Acts 16 – 'acted as if she were filled with the Holy Spirit'.
We learn that she did 'certain astonishing and extraordinary
things'. She even predicted the future, prophesying (somewhat ironically) her own downfall! Eventually, however, after
leading several clergy astray, an exorcist confronted her and,
over a period of time, managed to get the motivating spirit
behind the woman's behaviour to reveal its true colours. The
exorcist, inspired by both his own unease and the exhortation
of many brothers who were present at the time, decided to act.
He realized – as many of us must do today – that not all that
glitters is necessarily gold in charismatic circles.

Criteria for Testing

One humbling lesson from the two stories told above is the
realization that Christians are as vulnerable to deception as
non-Christians. Paul and Silas did not act straight away in the
context of the slave-girl. They were evidently unsure, as we

would have been. Furthermore, the church leaders in the story told by Firmilian did not act for a considerable length of time in the context of the pseudo-prophetess. Most of them were totally taken in by the woman's apparent credibility and authority. What these incidents highlight is the need for proper, thorough criteria for distinguishing spirits. This is particularly so in times of revival, when *pneumatika* or 'spiritual phenomena' (I Corinthians 12:1) are very much in evidence. So what are the proper criteria for discernment? How do we assess what is holy, human or unholy in origin?

In I John 4:1, the apostle John writes to his beloved flock that they are not to believe every spirit but rather test the spirits to see if they are from God. In the verses following this exhortation there are some guidelines for testing *pneumata* which, if combined with those found in I Corinthians 12-14, can furnish us with some rigorous, Biblical criteria for discernment. There are three primary ones, and I call these the test of Christology, the test of character and the test of consequence.

First of all, the test of Christology (Christology means our understanding and appreciation of Jesus Christ). If a spiritual manifestation is motivated by the Holy Spirit, then we can be sure that it will result in Jesus of Nazareth being exalted as Lord. In I Corinthians 12:3, Paul states that 'No one can say "Jesus is Lord", except by the Holy Spirit'. The earliest Christian creed consisted of the confession, 'Jesus is Lord'. In other words, people who became converts to Christianity exclaimed their deep conviction that the human being known as Jesus of Nazareth was *kurios*, the word translated 'Lord', and which was used of Yahweh in the Greek translation of the Old Testament. What Paul is saying in I Corinthians 12:3 is that the primary function of the Holy Spirit is to inspire people to declare that the earthly Jesus is Lord. When the historical Jesus – the Jesus born to Mary, who taught and ministered in Palestine, who died on the Cross and who rose from the dead – is truly exalted as 'Lord and Christ', there we can guarantee that the Holy Spirit is at work. As the apostle John was to say a few decades later, 'This is how you can recognize the Spirit of

God: Every spirit that acknowledges that Jesus Christ has come in the flesh is of God.' That, in brief, is the test of Christology.

John adds a further test, as does Paul. Both of them emphasize the test of character. They both encourage us to ask, 'What is the character of this spirit?' In particular, 'Does it have the character of *agape* about it?' 'Does it arise from and promote Christ-like love?' John, we should note, has several fundamental criteria for helping his congregations to be sure that they are Christians. The first is whether or not they believe that Jesus is the Son of God. The second is whether or not they love the brethren. If they do both, they can be certain that they belong to God:

> And this is his command: to believe in the name of his Son,
> and to love one another as he commanded us (I John 3:23).

The second is important when we consider the test of character. Paul too emphasizes the importance of love in the context of charismatic phenomena. He does this by placing a fine eulogy of Christ-like love between the two chapters in I Corinthians which deal with *pneumatika* or spiritual phenomena. Love is a very important word to Paul, occurring some 75 times in his letters. Paul's teaching in I Corinthians 12-14 is unavoidably clear.: if a charismatic experience is truly inspired by God, then love will be the chief quality visible in the character of the recipient. When a spiritual manifestation promotes a radical and active love of God and for others, then that experience is to be welcomed. That, in brief, is the test of character.

The third criterion for discernment is the test of consequence. In Matthew 7:15-16, Jesus himself warned:

> Watch out for false prophets. They come to you in sheep's
> clothing, but inwardly they are ferocious wolves. By their fruit
> you will recognize them.

Jesus cautioned the disciples not to be gullible, credulous and vulnerable to deception. He promised that false prophets would appear in their communities. People with a deceptively authoritative charisma would emerge in their churches. They were to be watched and assessed. How were they to be evaluated? By the consequences of their ministry. If the consequence was 'good fruit' (Matthew 7:17) they would be welcomed. If the consequence was 'bad fruit' they would be disciplined. What, then, constitutes 'good fruit'? For Paul in I Corinthians the word he chooses to describe good fruit is *oikodome*, meaning literally 'building up'. The church is like a spiritual temple. It is being built up on the earth as the years go by. Everything which results in the church being built up can be regarded as inspired by the Holy Spirit. If such things heal relationships, strengthen unity, build up the body of Christ, then they are of God. That, in brief, is the test of consequence.

Testing the Spirits

Having provided a Biblical theology of discernment we are now in a position to return to the subject of the Toronto blessing and ask, 'Is this a work of the Holy Spirit or not?' Straight away we need to address an important issue which is one to do with time. The truth of the matter is that insufficient time has elapsed for us to say with complete conviction that a mighty work of God's Holy Spirit has taken place and is taking place. A reasonable length of time (at least one year, I would say) is necessary for us to employ the test of consequence. In other words, the blessing must be allowed to take root and bear fruit before we can properly assess its authenticity and its holiness. Take for example the following testimony from the era of the Charismatic renewal in the 1960s. The story is told by the Rev. Philip Smith, a retired vicar, who was one of the first people to be radically impacted by the experience which he calls 'baptism in the Holy Spirit'. The words which you are about to read are taken from the magazine known as *Logos* (1964, Vol. III, no. 2, pp. 26-7) and describe the experience which occurred to Philip on September 28th 1962:

> . . . in September 1962 our organist arrived in the vestry one
> Sunday morning with the news 'I have been baptized in the
> Holy Ghost.' We had least expected it from him – such a solid
> Church of England Christian! His life and witness was
> immediately different. There was no denying the joy and
> power, and the uplifting of the Lord Jesus.
>   As we went through the relevant Scriptures, the Lord
> showed us that this was his gift, offered to every one of his
> children, and that since the Holy Spirit had been outpoured at
> Pentecost there was no longer any need to 'wait', but to
> *believe* and *receive*. On September 28, 1962, my wife and I
> therefore received the Baptism of the Holy Ghost, through
> the laying on of hands with prayer. In every case there has
> been the initial evidence of tongues, and the keynote of
> praise. Praising heart and praising lips (p. 27).

That is a beautiful testimony told with childlike humility. It is
hard not to fall to one's knees in adoration of the Lord when
reading it. However, the temptation to respond too quickly
must be resisted. The fact is, we need to ask the simple question, 'What fruit did this experience bear? What were the long-
term consequences?' Fortunately, in this kind of case, we are on
much firmer ground than with the Toronto blessing. Recently
I visited Philip Smith to ask him about the differences this
experience had made to the subsequent thirty years of his
Christian life. Whilst he spoke to me of that experience, tears
came to his eyes. It became quickly clear, exactly thirty years
on, that this experience was still fresh in his memory and very
dear to his heart. Indeed, later on he sent me a letter which
underlined this truth, and which also bears testimony to the
profound fruit in Philip's own life. He wrote this of the
primary fruit of his experience:

> The Holy Spirit glorifies and magnifies (literally and
> metaphorically) Jesus in our own lives (John 16:14). I believe

this is achieved especially when we praise in tongues; as we send the glory 'up', He sends the glory 'down' upon us, and we see the 'bigness' of our Lord Jesus and the smallness of our problems and of ourselves. Thus you edify yourself, build yourself up, and become a stronger Christian.

In other words, the greatest, most lasting consequence of Philip's experience was the fact that it began a lifestyle of glorifying, exalting and adoring the Lord Jesus Christ. That the experience of spiritual renewal in 1962 was directly responsible for this is evident from his words just before the paragraph cited above:

It was my privilege to share with you some aspects of that miraculous outpouring of God's Holy Spirit upon us 30 years ago. How great and wonderful, merciful and patient is our God, our loving Heavenly Father!

Thirty years on, Philip is still praising God, still glorifying Christ, still living a life wholly devoted to the Lord. There can be *no* doubt that his experience of charismatic renewal was authentic and godly. Only the worst cynic would suggest otherwise.

When we address the experiences associated with the Toronto blessing, we are not able to be as confident as this because less time has elapsed between people's experiences and the long-term consequences. Having said that, however, the early signs are positive; in other words, that the Toronto blessing is a work of the Holy Spirit which will bear very significant fruit in innumerable churches. Let us have an example of such fruitfulness. The testimony which follows is from a woman called Carol, who attends my church here in Sheffield and who has recently visited Toronto with her husband Tim. Her story is typical of the many others I have heard and received. I can vouch for the truthfulness of this narrative, and also for the credibility of the narrator.

Carol Fordham:

The thing that struck me most about my experience in Toronto was God's perfect provision for each individual. I saw the Holy Spirit intervene powerfully to break down barriers in dramatic ways. For some through uncontrollable laughing, roaring, jerking and shaking. For others the Lord brought emotional release gently through tears and resting in his arms.

I had never before experienced such a balance between being a part of the whole world-wide Church and a unique and precious child of God. The sense of God's sovereignty was immense and made my experience of his love for me even more amazing. It was an intense awareness of his special attention to the circumstances of my life and my individual needs.

We visited the Vineyard Church on three occasions and God chose to minister to me from his father heart on the first night, through Jesus' love on the second and to anoint me with the Holy Spirit on the third. When I was prayed for it was as if God shone a spotlight on the deep need he wanted to address. Without a word from me the ministry team spoke God's love and comfort into the particular need, using words from Scripture that were special promises to me and that had been used to unlock emotional pain through prayer in the past. It was as though God was reminding me of what he had done to bring me to this point and then he went beyond it to give me more healing and wholeness in a deeper relationship with him.

On the first night God loved and healed the broken little girl inside and enabled me to fall into his arms of security and comfort. On the second I had a very powerful experience of Jesus' love. I felt waves of love wash over me, rocking me back and forth. It was also like oil being poured onto my head and running down my back and chest and arms and legs. During this experience I was released from emotional pain through tears.

I felt a sense of worthiness that came from Jesus that I had not known before and that freed me from guilt, shame and self-condemnation. Because I recognized that Jesus had clothed me in robes or righteousness I was able to open myself to him in a way I could not before and be led by him into a deeper relationship with him, into 'water up to my waist' (Ezekiel 47:4). Once this had taken place Jesus set me apart and anointed my hands for healing. He filled me with his joy and I fell over in fits of giggles, it was like being tickled on the inside.

On the third night I received confirmation of what had been happening. A stranger prayed for me and again I was anointed by the Holy Spirit to bring healing, to bind up the broken-hearted and set captives free (Isaiah 61:1). I was released from fear of men and reminded that the Lord had anointed me and he would do it. I felt a new strength and confidence through this prayer.

Since these experiences I have felt a new expectancy to hear from God, a deeper awareness of his love, a greater love from Jesus and a new ability to minister his love to others. I also feel a greater confidence in the church as I see God refreshing and restoring his people.

If we are to be confident that this kind of experience is a work of the Holy Spirit, we must map it against the three criteria described earlier: the test of Christology, the test of character, the test of consequence.

First of all, then, we consider the test of Christology. Is this experience one in which the recipient is moved to a greater level of awareness of the reality, the nature and the Lordship of Jesus Christ? The simple answer to that is 'yes'! The whole experience is emphatically Christ-centred. In fact, if you read carefully, you will see that it is thoroughly Trinitarian: a new sense of the healing love of God the Father, the saving grace of God the Son, and the awesome power of God the Holy Spirit. What could be more Christian than that? Indeed, I have seen a profound change in Carol, from a cynical detachment and resistance to worship, to a most intense desire to adore God at every possible opportunity.

Secondly, we consider the test of character – specifically whether or not the experience promotes Christ-like love. The answer to that is again a very definite 'yes'! The whole narrative is soaked in divine love. Carol writes with deep feeling of the love which she received from God and the love which she felt moved, as a consequence, to share with others. I can bear witness to the difference in Carol. Whereas before she tended to be an individual in church, now she is truly a member of the body of Christ, genuinely concerned for the wellbeing of others, and profoundly moved by the suffering which so many both inside and outside the church are experiencing.

Thirdly, we consider the test of consequence. In a sense we have already begun to touch on the fruit of Carol's experiences in Toronto. But it is worth listing what they are: a new sense of intimacy with the Father, wholeness in the Son, effectiveness in the Spirit. There is certainly a new freedom in her worship, a new excitement about what God is doing in his church, and a fresh zeal for practical service to others.

Given these responses to the three tests mentioned above, how can we say anything else but that this is the Lord's work, and it is marvellous in our eyes! Indeed, who else could it be? What on earth could the evil one gain from such a positive and marked transformation? How on earth could a person like Carol have engineered such a radical change in her own strength alone? The fact that this story is representative of the vast majority of a huge and growing number of testimonies means that we are left with no alternative but to say that the Toronto blessing is indeed the Lord's work. 'The Lord is here!', to quote the punch-line of the story told at the start of this chapter. Even if we cannot have the luxury of the kind of hindsight which Philip Smith's story gives us, the truth of the matter is that such testimonies are signs of a major new work of the Holy Spirit of God.

But is this Revival?

I hope that all my readers are happy to agree with this evaluation on Biblical and theological grounds – even allowing for some of the more carnal and excessive elements in the current context. But this still leaves the second of the two main questions set for this chapter. If the first was to do with discerning whether this is God or not, the second has to do with defining what kind of work this is? In particular, we need to ask whether or not the Toronto blessing constitutes a revival, or at the least, the first indications of an impending revival.

Answering that question of course depends upon our understanding of revival. In my opinion, a revival is a restoration of the people of God to the reality of Pentecost – i.e., a profound sense of God's presence in worship, a new holiness of life, true and authentic community, and a potent effectiveness in reaching out to the lost. It is, in short, a restoration of the body of Christ to the pattern and power of Pentecost. In this respect I agree wholeheartedly with the great preacher D. L. Moody, who said of the Holy Spirit:

> See how he came on the Day of Pentecost! It is not carnal to pray that he may come again and that the place may be shaken. I believe that Pentecost was but a specimen day. I think the Church has made this woeful mistake that Pentecost was a miracle never to be repeated. I have thought too that Pentecost was a miracle that is not to be repeated. I believe now if we looked on Pentecost as a specimen day and began to pray, we should have the old Pentecostal fire here in Boston.

Defining revival as a restoration of the pattern and power of Pentecost implies that the people of God go through troughs of spiritual recession prior to that restoration. This is indeed the case. As an illustration of this tendency of God's people to move from recession to restoration, let us turn to the Book of Judges. It just so happens that we as a church at St Mark's have spent the better part of a year in Judges 6-7, the story of Gideon. In setting the scene for these sermons, we have looked closely at Judges chapter 2, which establishes the necessary background for the whole book. In Judges 2, the narrator tells us that after Joshua's death, a whole generation arose who did not know the Lord and who had no knowledge of what the Lord had done for Israel. That phrase, 'did not know the Lord', is immensely significant. In the Old Testament, the Hebrew word for 'knowing' is *yada*, the same word which is used in Genesis 4:1 where the writer says that Adam 'knew' his wife Eve; i.e. had sexual intercourse with her. *Yada*-knowledge is therefore intimate, unitive, personal knowledge. When the storyteller in Judges 2:10 says that a generation emerged which did not 'know' God, that means that they did not know Yahweh personally, deeply, subjectively – in their hearts as well as in their heads. They neither had a personal relationship with the Lord, nor did they know about his great and marvellous deeds in the relatively recent past.

What happens next is that the people of God, as a direct consequence of their ignorance of God, did evil in the eyes of the Lord (Judges 2:11). Seven times in the Book of Judges this is said of the people of Israel – they did evil, they disobeyed, they departed from God's ways. This starts a cycle (repeated seven times between Judges 3:7 and 16:31) in which the Israelites fall into rebellion. This rebellion is usually expressed in the form of idolatry, of following and worshipping the pagan gods of the tribes around them in Canaan (Judges 2:12-13). The net result of this is that God's people fall into a spiritual, moral and socio-economic recession. This recession is directly caused by the Lord himself, who hands his people over to marauding oppressors (Judges 2:14-15). These oppressors cause the people of Israel great grief, particularly in the form of material poverty. In this state of desolation, they move into a third phase of the cycle: repentance. They groan under their affliction and cry out to the Lord in their distress. This leads to the fourth stage of the cycle, restoration. God sends a judge or a liberator to rescue his people (Judges 2:18) and to bring them back to a way of life based on the written covenant (Judges 2:1-5). Looked at as a whole, this cycle, which occurs seven times in the Book of Judges, looks like this:

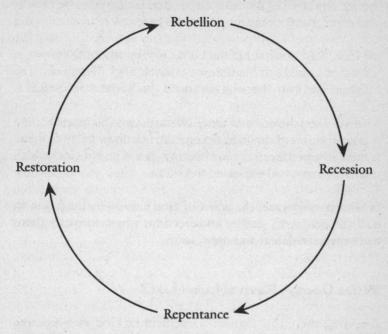

Using this cycle as a guide (and no more than that), I would like to propose that revivals are essentially extraordinary works of God's grace. They are periods of time in which God mercifully restores his people after they have fallen from a relationship with him based on *yada*-knowledge. The Lord does this work of revival by raising three things; first of all, the level of his people's awareness concerning their sin (usually through people anointed with a prophetic gift, see Judges 6:7-10); secondly, by raising up charismatic leaders known as judges; thirdly, by raising his people from a powerless minority into a powerful army. In this process of revival, the Holy Spirit – as in every revival – plays the key role. We should note in particular the way in which the Spirit of God empowers the judges to do the work which leads to the restoration of Israel's fortunes:

3:9: The Spirit of the Lord came upon Othniel, so that he became Israel's judge and went to war.

6:34: The Spirit of the Lord came upon Gideon, and he blew a trumpet, summoning the Abiezrites to follow him . . .

11:29: Then the Spirit of the Lord came upon Jephthah. He crossed Gilead and Manasseh, passed through Mizpah of Gilead, and from there he advanced against the Ammonites.

14:19: Then the Spirit of the Lord came upon Samson in power. He went down to Askelon, struck down thirty of their men, stripped them of their belongings and gave their clothes to those who had explained the riddle.

In almost every case, the Spirit of God empowers the judge to lead the people to victory and freedom where formerly there had only been defeat and oppression.

What Does A Revival Look Like?

A revival, then, is a massive movement of God in which the Church is visited by the Holy Spirit, and radically transformed from compromise to holiness, from inertia to action, from weakness to strength. It is, in short, a restoration of the Church to the pattern and power of Pentecost. Having said that, I am not suggesting from my analysis of the Book of Judges that this transformation always occurs in the exact manner described there. That kind of generalization would effectively turn the whole of church history into a deterministic, cyclical pattern of rebellion, recession, repentance and restoration. What I am suggesting is that revivals have occurred during periods of intense and widespread recession both within the Church and within the world. They have usually occurred when God's people have been crying out to the Lord in their impoverishment (Judges 6:6) – an impoverishment which often consists of spiritual, moral and economic bankruptcy. As the Church gets on its knees before the sovereign Lord of the universe and repents with godly sorrow, the Lord is pleased to send the refining fire of his Holy Spirit to his people in order to transform a weak ghetto-minority into a bold and effective community.

Very few of us are privileged enough to have witnessed a revival. Nevertheless, there are historical, eye-witness records of seasons which have been described as revivals. In what follows I will refer to two sources in order to describe some distinctives of revival: first of all, the story of Pentecost in Acts 2 (which furnishes us with the archetype, if you will, of all revivals); secondly, R. B. Jones' simple description of the Welsh Revival of 1904 (entitled *Rent Heavens*). From these two sources -- one from the first century, the other from the twentieth century -- we learn that revivals have the following distinctives:

1 Revivals are always God's initiative not ours
In Acts 2, the disciples were told to wait for the Holy Spirit by Jesus. They did not know when the power would come from heaven. That was up to the Father, who sets the times and dates for such events by his own authority (Acts 1:7). When the Holy Spirit did come upon them (Acts 2:1-4), it was the Father who decided that it should happen, and it was the ascended Lord Jesus who gave the gift. Jesus was and is the Baptizer in the Holy Spirit (Acts 1:5). True revivals therefore have the Father as their source, the Son as their agency, and the Spirit as their instrument.

R. B. Jones draws attention to this divine initiative by helpfully distinguishing between a mission and a revival. He writes:

> A mission has a human leader; a mission is organized. Revival, on the other hand, has but one Leader – the Holy Spirit; Revival is never organized. It is energy, without man-made machinery. To use another's words, 'True Revival is never *worked up*; it always *comes down* from above'.

When the Revival hit Wales, it was certainly felt as a divine visitation – as something that had come down from heaven rather than something which had been worked up on earth.

2 Revivals do, however, follow pleading to God in prayer
Acts 1:14 reveals that the Pentecost event was preceded by a season marked for its on-going, corporate prayer:

> They all joined together constantly in prayer, along with the women and Mary the mother of Jesus, and with his brothers.

In Acts 2:1, when the day of Pentecost arrives, the disciples are all together in one place. If this was the Temple, then it is likely that they were in prayer (Luke 24:53).

Prayer, then, preceded Pentecost. What of the Welsh Revival? Jones makes it clear that 'no Revival is of sudden origin'. As he explains, 'Behind the startling outburst is a process which sometimes goes on for years, a purifying and preparatory process' (p. 22). In particular, Jones draws attention to the hidden spring of prayer prior to the Welsh Revival. Indeed, he notes that

> God seems to have so ordained that most, if not indeed all, of his activities in the moral and spiritual realms should be the responses of his heart and power to the prayers of his people. No axiom seems surer than that.

However, Jones also confesses a difficulty with regard to this principle as it relates to the Welsh Revival. For whilst there were doubtless many people pleading for Revival in the years prior to 1904, Jones himself admits that he is not conscious from his own memory or from the historical records of a 'form of adequate prayer that might explain the copious showers that fell' (p. 22). Thus, even though we may say that revivals occur after periods of intense prayer, the extraordinary blessings which are received are deemed far greater than what the preparatory prayer could ever have merited. Revivals, in short, are acknowledged as undeserved – in short, as grace.

3 Revivals are intimately connected with the exaltation of Jesus Christ

In Acts 1:9, Jesus is taken up into heaven before the very eyes of the disciples. The direct consequence of this ascension is ongoing adoration of Jesus. Luke 24:52 informs us that the disciples who witnessed this extraordinary event 'worshipped him and returned to Jerusalem with great joy'.

It seems that there is some relationship between the church's adoration of Christ and the Father's release of the Spirit. It is almost as if the praise of Christ goes up so that the gift of God comes down. Witness the following incident which occurred just before the Welsh Revival:

> Earlier in the year – in February, so runs the story – at a meeting of young Endeavourers, a young girl was lifted from her seat, and in spite of her natural and pronounced shyness, with trembling lips was inspired to say fervently in Welsh, 'Yr wyf yn caru Iesu Grist a'm holl galon' ('I love Jesus Christ with all of my heart'). It was all so unexpected, so beautifully simple and sincere, so manifestly of the Spirit that it acted like a spark on tinder. The weeks that followed were unforgettable and, in August 1904, after several months, as the writer himself saw, the fire burned brightly.

There is therefore a mysterious relationship between the lifting up of Jesus and the pouring down of the Holy Spirit. Certainly, once a true revival is underway, ongoing adoration of Jesus Christ is a marked feature. Sometimes the works of the Holy Spirit inevitably become the centre of attention. When that happens, wise leaders are quick to emphasize the view expressed by Frank Bartleman during the Los Angeles Revival in 1906:

> In the beginning of the 'Pentecostal' work I became very much exercised in the Spirit that Jesus should not be slighted, 'lost in the temple', by the exaltation of the Holy Ghost, and of the

'gifts' of the Spirit. There seemed great danger of losing sight
of the fact that Jesus was 'all, and in all'. I endeavoured to keep
him as the central theme and figure before the people. Jesus
should be the centre of our preaching. All comes through and
in him. The Holy Ghost is given to 'show the things of Christ'.
The work of Calvary, the atonement, must be the centre for
our consideration. The Holy Ghost never draws our attention
from Christ to himself, but rather reveals Christ in a fuller way.

In every true revival, Jesus is exalted as 'both Lord and Christ'
(Acts 2:36).

4 Revivals are accompanied by extraordinary phenomena
When the Holy Spirit fell down upon the disciples on the day
of Pentecost, there were some highly unusual manifestations of
the Spirit. There was a sound like the blowing of a violent
wind, and there was a sighting of what looked like tongues of
fire alighting upon each of the disciples. The whole house
where the disciples were sitting was filled with the powerful
presence of the Holy Spirit, and the disciples started speaking
in unlearnt foreign languages as a result. In fact, they behaved
so oddly that some of the onlookers thought they were drunk
(Acts 2:13). Thereafter, manifestations of the Holy Spirit were
frequently witnessed. Indeed, Luke informs us that many
wonders and miraculous signs were done by the apostles in the
first Pentecostal community (Acts 2:43).

There are always unusual phenomena during revivals, as we
shall see in the following chapters. In the history books you will
find countless reports of strange physical and emotional
responses by people to the awesome presence of God in meeting
halls and churches. Jones, in his analysis of the Welsh Revival,
cautions us not to take these phenomena too seriously. Incidents
of such phenomena are purely *incidental*, thrilling and impres-
sive though they may be. Nevertheless, they can be dramatic.
Jones records one incident which occurred just after he had
preached a sermon on Anglesey in the first months of 1905:

As one man, first with a sigh of relief, and, then, with a delirious shout of joy, the whole huge audience sprang to their feet. The vision had completely overwhelmed them and, one is not ashamed to tell it, for a moment they were beside themselves with heavenly joy. The speaker never realized anything like it anywhere. The whole place at that moment was so awful with the glory of God – one uses the word 'awful' deliberately; the holy presence of God was so manifested that the speaker himself was overwhelmed; the pulpit where he stood was so filled with the light of God that he had to withdraw!

The unusual phenomena which attend revivals – shaking, delirious shouts of joy, drunken behaviour, falling over, and so on – are commonplace enough. *They are physical, emotional and cultural reactions to the powerful presence of the Holy Spirit.* They are effects not causes. As such, they should not be over-valued or overemphasized.

5 Revivals result in continuous and exuberant praise
Obviously Pentecost produced a rich outbreak of praise on the part of the disciples. They all started speaking out the wonders of God in unlearnt languages, and at the same time! Later on, these same disciples are still 'praising God' (Acts 2:47).

In the Welsh Revival, praise was dominant. Jones reports that 'a notable feature was the audible praying of many at one and the same time, and that without producing the slightest sense of confusion'. He also writes:

The singing was truly magnificent and stirring. Welsh congregational singing is something unique. In the places of worship the singing is not entrusted to a few who compose the choir. The whole congregation *is* the choir ... In the Revival meetings there was no human leader. There was no hymn book; no one gave out a hymn. Anybody started the singing. And, very rarely did it happen that the hymn started, no one knew by whom, was out of harmony with the mood of the meeting at the moment.

6 Revivals always impact the globe, centrifugally – as it were
Revivals always start in a small geographical area but then
spread like wildfire to the continents of the world. This international consequence is partly hinted at in the story of Pentecost in Acts 2:5-11, where Luke reels off a long list of the
ethnic groups who were in Jerusalem for the festival and who
witnessed the outpouring of the Holy Spirit. It is certainly
explicitly stated in Acts 1:8 where Jesus prophesies that the
disciples will be his witnesses first in Jerusalem, then in Judea,
then in Samaria, to the ends of the earth.

Thus there is a kind of centrifugal quality about revival. A
centrifugal movement is one in which momentum proceeds
from a small centre in an outward direction, thus:

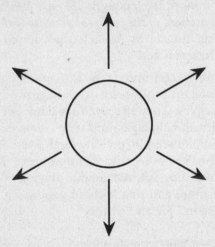

In the Welsh Revival, this centrifugal movement is clearly
visible, with pastors and missionaries in particular visiting from
all over the world and then carrying the flame back to the
counties and countries from which they had come. Similarly,
many people who were converted went out from Wales as
missionaries to the ends of the earth. Jones recorded the names
of hundreds of men and women whom he knew had left for the
mission field as a direct result of the Welsh Revival.

7 The location of a revival also has a marked centripetal effect
As large numbers of people flow out from a small geographical
centre to the ends of the earth, so large numbers of people flow
into that centre – in a centripetal movement, as it were – from
all over the globe. This centripetal movement looks like this:

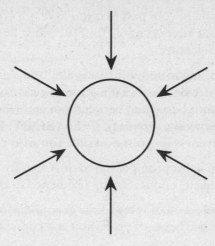

This kind of movement is certainly described by Jones in his
account of the Welsh Revival. It is also a marked feature of the
birth of the Pentecostal movement. Thus, Frank Bartleman
noted the following about the Asuza Street Revival:

> God was working mightily. It seemed that everyone had to go
> to 'Asuza'. Missionaries were gathered there from Africa,
> India, and the islands of the sea. Preachers and workers had
> crossed the continent, and came from distant islands, with an
> irresistible drawing to Los Angeles.

8 Revivals lead to the effective preaching of the Gospel
After the Holy Spirit has baptized the disciples in Acts 2:1-13,
Peter then stands up and preaches the Gospel to a huge crowd.
At the end of this sermon, 3000 people are converted (Acts
2:41) as they come to an awareness of their sinfulness on the

one hand (Acts 2:36), and God's gracious provision of forgiveness, through Jesus, on the other (Acts 2:38-9).

In the early days of the Welsh Revival, the key figure – Evan Roberts – used to preach at length on the following 'Four Points' (as they became known):

1 Is there any sin in your past that you have not confessed to God? On your knees at once. Your past must be put away, and yourself cleansed.

2 Is there anything in your life that is doubtful – anything that you cannot decide whether it is good or evil? Away with it. There must not be a cloud between you and God. Have you forgiven everybody, *everybody*, EVERYBODY? If not, don't expect forgiveness for your own sins. You won't get it.

3 Do what the Spirit prompts you to do. Obedience – prompt, implicit, unquestioning obedience to the Spirit.

4 A public confession of Jesus Christ as your Saviour. There is a vast difference between profession and confession.

This kind of direct, challenging and uncluttered preaching of the Gospel is a feature of revivals.

9 Related to this, revivals evoke an acute consciousness of
    human sin

In Acts 2, the result of Peter's sermon is that the people were 'cut to the heart' when they heard his words. Many are the stories of this kind of conviction in revival meetings. Jones records the following incident, when he himself was preaching in a large, crowded chapel in 1905:

> The theme of the message was Isaiah, Chapter Six. The light of God's holiness was turned upon the hearts and lives of those present. Conviction of sin, and of its terrible desert, was so crushing that a feeling of almost despair grew over all hearts. So grievous a thing was sin; so richly and inevitably did it deserve the severest judgement of God, that hearts questioned, Could God forgive? Could God cleanse? Then

came the word about the altar, the tongs, and the live coal
touching the confessedly vile lips, and the gracious and
complete removal of their vileness. After all, there was hope!
God was forgiving, and he had cleansing for the worst. When
the rapt listeners realized all this the effect was – well,
'electrifying' is far too weak a word; it was absolutely beyond
any metaphor to describe it.

The awful realization of our sins, followed by the rapturous
recognition of God's forgiveness, is a constant theme of
revivals.

10 Revivals produce large numbers of converts
In Acts 2:41 it is said that 3000 were added to the church in
one day. In Acts 2:47, Luke tells us that 'the Lord added to
their number daily those who were being saved'. This kind of
growth through evangelism and conversion is common in
revivals. Jones writes of the Welsh Revival:

There were, of course, thousands upon thousands of cases of
conversion from the ranks of the irreligious. 'Broken
earthenware', in large numbers, were re-shaped in the Divine
Potter's hands. Magistrates, court advocates, and the police
were given a real holiday; their occupation being almost
altogether gone. Characters sunken in vice and crime, such as
the law could neither regenerate nor control, nor indeed even
intimidate, found transformation through the grace and truth
which came by Jesus Christ.

Elsewhere, Jones puts the figure of those converted during the
Welsh Revival in the region of 100,000. Indeed, he remarks
that 'a *small* church became a rarity in the land'.

11 Revivals result in a hunger for the Word of God
In Acts 2:42 we learn that the first converts after Pentecost
were 'devoted' to the apostles' teaching. That teaching would
have included elements which are now part of what we call the

Bible – Old Testament Scriptures which looked forward to Jesus, the teachings of Jesus himself, as well as stories about his life told by eyewitnesses. To this the new Christians were 'devoted'. They were not just interested in this teaching, they were hungry for it. They were eager to hear it.

The same sort of desire for the Word of God was evident during the Welsh Revival, as is made clear from Jones' remark that

> There was an intense hunger for the Word, and the awakened ones could not tolerate anything but the Word, and that too spoken by those who had personal experience of its power in their own hearts and lives.

Later, Jones remarks that

> . . . it [the Revival] made every one read his Bible. It was to many almost a re-discovery of the old Book. And people now read it for practical purposes. Young Christian workers, for example, were anxious to learn how rightly to dispense the truth to needy souls . . . The supplies of Scriptures from the B. & F.B.S. alone during November and December 1904, more than trebled those of the corresponding period in the previous year.

12 Revivals lead to a profound unity between Spirit-filled believers

In Acts 2:42, the members of the church of Pentecost devote themselves not only to the Word but also to *koinonia*, to fellowship. This new sense of community, of fellowship in and through the Holy Spirit, is a particularly marked feature of revivals. In particular, revivals break down walls of social and denominational prejudice. Thus, an old miner, speaking of the feuds between Unionists and Non-unionists at the collieries, told a journalist in 1905:

> I have seen neighbours refuse to speak to each other, although

they had been great friends. I have seen some refuse to
descend the mine in the same cage with men who did not
belong to the Federation, or to speak to them who did not
belong to the Federation, or to speak to them below ground,
except with an oath. The Revival has stopped all that, and
colliers look upon each other, in spite of all the differences, as
friends and companions. Some of the Non-unionists were
among the best of men, and, at the meeting I have just left,
one of them was leading the prayers, and Unionists joining in!

As Jones puts it, 'The one Spirit of God, when poured out,
puts an end to sectionalism and suspicion'. A true, united
community is born in genuine revivals. Old differences are
buried. A new spirit of generosity is made manifest (Acts 2:45).
Indeed, truly can it be said that 'all the believers have everything in common' (Acts 2:44).

13 Revivals bring about a remarkable renewal of prayer
In Acts 2:42, Luke tells us that the church of Pentecost was
devoted also to prayer. This too is a noticeable consequence of
revivals. Jones wrote

Praying mingled largely with praising. And, such praying!
Praying which rent the heavens; praying that secured
immediate and marvellous answers. It startled one to hear the
very young and unlettered pray with such unction, diction, and
intelligence as could only be accounted for in one way. Filled
with the Spirit, they were utterly beyond themselves in vision,
thought and expression.

14 Revivals always create a sense of awe at God's holy and
pervasive presence
In Acts 2:43, Luke says that 'everyone was filled with awe',
mainly because of the extraordinarily powerful sense of God's
presence manifested in signs and wonders. Here again we may
note what Jones reports concerning the Welsh Revival. He
wrote:

If one were asked to describe in a word the outstanding feature of those days, one would unhesitatingly reply that *it was the universal, inescapable sense of the presence of God.*

Jones cites the following instance of this:

A sense of the Lord's presence was everywhere. It pervaded, nay, it created the spiritual atmosphere. It mattered not where one went the consciousness of the reality and the nearness of God followed. Felt, of course, in the Revival gatherings, it was by no means confined to them; it was also felt in the homes, on the streets, in the mines and factories, in the schools, yea, and even in the theatres and drinking-saloons. The strange result was that wherever people gathered became a place of awe ... (p. 41).

15 In revivals, people cannot stop meeting in order to encounter God
One of the most noticeable consequences of what Jones calls 'remarkable periodical of sheddings-forth of the Holy Spirit in power' is the fact that people meet continuously to be in the Lord's presence. This was the case, of course, at Pentecost, where Luke reports that

Every day they continued to meet together in the temple courts (Acts 2:46).

Jones reports of the Welsh Revival that

Morning, afternoon and evening meetings were held each day, and, frequently, meetings were much prolonged.

Indeed, Jones repeats a marvellous comment from a person who had been present at the Ulster Revival in 1859:

The difficulty used to be to get the people *into* the church, but the difficulty now is to get them *out.*

16 Revivals produce a much higher level of financial giving
Luke says of the earliest church members that

> Selling their possessions and goods, they gave to anyone as he
> had need (Acts 2:45).

Jones draws attention to this kind of material altruism as well.
He reports that

> As remarkable a feature as any was that upon which the late
> Lord Pontypridd thus remarked, 'The Revival finances itself.
> There are no bills, no halls, no salaries'.

17 Revivals produce beneficial effects in the wider community
Another way of putting this is as follows: when the Holy Spirit
revives the church, the church starts to be a blessing to the
community. The name of the Lord and the name of the church
cease to become a reproach and begin to be a blessing. What
we read in Acts 2:47 becomes a reality in today's experience –
that the first Christians found favour with all the people. The
primary reason for this lies in the radical, positive changes
throughout whole communities. Thus Jones says of Wales in
1904

> What would readily be regarded as an undoubted 'practical'
> result was the Revival's effect in the matter of 'strikes'.
> Bethesda, North Wales, the centre of the widely known and
> protracted bitter 'Penrhyn Strike', had for years suffered
> acutely from the social, domestic, and religious dis-union
> which that struggle occasioned. Families and churches were
> rent in the unfortunate dispute, and life-long friendships
> shattered. So bitter were the divisions, that many qualified to
> judge said that there could be no restoration within that
> generation. The Revival came; and, with it, a transformation as
> complete as it was sudden. Women who sued one another in
> the courts, prayed side by side in the same meeting! Members
> of families who had not spoken to each other for years met in

cordial love. In one fortnight the normal order of things had been restored by the power of God. Feuds and differences were forgotten; peace and harmony took the place of discord and enmity.

18 Revivals lead to a sense of the imminence of the Parousia Only a brief comment is required here. It is a well known fact that Peter alters the prophecy from Joel which he cites at the start of his sermon in Acts 2:17. Where Joel had 'After these things', Peter puts 'In the last days'. This sense of the imminence of the end of the world and the Parousia or return of Jesus Christ always occurs when there is a great outpouring of the Holy Spirit. Jones says of his own experience during the Welsh Revival:

> The writer's own testimony is but an instance of that of thousands. Never can he forget the occasion, the place, nor the day when, alone with God, the truth flashed into his heart. He had heard no preaching, nor had he read any book on the subject; he simply shared the somewhat derisive attitude of others to a matter he knew nothing about beyond the mere name. At that moment, however, a conviction was wrought in his deepest heart that the Lord was coming; that he was coming quickly; that indeed he *must* come, and that, apart from his coming, there seemed no hope for the world.

Is the Toronto Blessing a Revival?

These eighteen snapshots of a genuine revival give us some criteria by which we can define the Toronto blessing. However, before we do so, a number of caveats need honestly to be borne in mind. First of all, we must allow for a degree of idealism in the narrative style of R. B. Jones. Jones is writing history as an eye-witness of the events, but his style is devotional and subjective. Whilst Luke's source is wholly authoritative, Jones' is only partially so. Secondly, we cannot put the Holy Spirit and sovereign work into neat and tidy categories. He is ofte characterized in terms of symbols which connote a wild, unmanageable and uncontainable nature – such as wind, fire and rivers of water. Advocating eighteen features of revival is not supposed to imply that we can control the ways of the Spirit. These characteristics are offered merely as a map, arrived at from inductive research from Acts 2 (primary source) and the revival in Wales (one of many secondary sources). Thirdly and finally, the Toronto blessing is still too young for us to assess with certainty whether or not it is a revival. What follows is only intended as a projection of present trends. They are merely some brief, general, and first impressions.

Let it be said at this stage that the early signs are that the Toronto blessing has many of the characteristics of a revival in the making. Reading the chronological records of events (see any of the many books on the Toronto blessing), it is clear that the extraordinary outpouring of the Holy Spirit upon the Vineyard Church at Toronto Airport was not a planned event but an unplanned, sovereign work of God. It was a work of divine not human initiative. It was preceded by a good deal of dependent prayer, particularly on the part of John Arnott and his church. One of the main features of this blessing, further-more, has been the centrality of Jesus Christ. The watchword has been Sarah Edwards' beautiful phrase about 'my dearness to Him [the Lord Jesus Christ] and His nearness to me'. Indeed, restoration of first love for the Lord has been commonplace. Furthermore, we should note the way in which praise has dominated the meetings where the Toronto blessing has been felt. Indeed, it has been for many of us as though 'the season of singing has come' (Song of Solomon 2:12). Remarkable also has been the ongoing evidence of unusual phenomena, such as roaring, fainting, shaking, laughing, drunken behaviour, and so on.

Other characteristics of revival are plainly visible. There is a marked centripetal movement, with many weary pastors, church leaders and missionaries flocking to Toronto from all over the world. There is a renewed hunger for the Word of God on the part of all those affected – not a renewal of cerebral study of the Bible but, as in all revivals, a renewed passion for hearing God today in and through the written words of Scripture. There has also been a noticeable work of reconciliation going on as a result of the Toronto blessing. Those affected have repaired broken relationships with other Christians. Walls of suspicion and division have been torn down. There has also been a very definite renewal of prayer, particularly intercessory prayer for the world and prophetic, listening prayer. Inside the halls and churches where these meetings have been held, there has been a constant expression of awe at what Gordon Fee has recently called 'God's empowering presence'. This has led many into a new sense of the Parousia. Another side effect of this is that hundreds of people have been returning night after night to the Toronto Vineyard Church – and to many other churches too – in order to experience this immanent sense of the transcendent and numinous Lord. As a result, like other revivals, this movement of the Spirit is 'financing itself'!

However, what we are not seeing at this stage is that centrifugal, evangelistic characteristic of revivals. The globe is not being impacted centrifugally with missionaries being called and sent out from Toronto (though many are returning to their own countries from Toronto as 'carriers of the blessing'). We have not seen this present movement, as yet, leading to a new, ubiquitous and effective preaching of the Gospel. Thus, there has been a greater emphasis upon joy and laughter than upon tears and conviction. As such, the widespread and acute consciousness of human sin on the part of non-Christians has not been obvious. The direct consequence of this lack of outer-directedness has predictably been an absence of item number ten on my list of revival characteristics ('large numbers of converts'), and also an absence of item number seventeen ('beneficial effects in the wider community'). To use the symbolism of Ezekiel 47:1-12, the river of the Spirit is still confined to the Temple courts – that is, to the churches. If this present move of God is to develop into a revival, then we must allow the Spirit to burst out of the closed doors of our churches and to carry us out into a world lost in the darkness of the Arabah. That, surely, is the challenge before us now.

FOR FURTHER STUDY

The following piece is a testimony from a conference evangelist in the Methodist Church, who was baptized in the Holy Spirit in the early 1960s.

I   Is this the kind of experience associated with revivals (understood as a restoration of the pattern and power of Pentecost)?

2   What does the test of Christology reveal?

3   What does the test of character reveal?

4   What does the test of consequence reveal?

5   Do you agree with Tyson's understanding of baptism in the Holy Spirit as 'the fulfilment of the new birth'?

6   Is the Toronto blessing resulting in similar or different experiences?

Fulfilment of the New Birth
Rev. Thomas Tyson:

Having been born and raised in a parsonage, the language of the Church was acquired in the natural course of events. I knew the words but not the Word. After finishing public high school and three semesters of college, I 'went out on my own'. This included work with the US Navy Department, three years of military service during World War II, coming home to marry my high school sweetheart and going into business. During this time, my ignorance of the Christian Faith left me with the conviction that it was impossible to be a Christian in a world like ours.

A young missionary came to our town during the Summer of 1947 to serve as an assistant for the Summer months. He was a likable person and we spent much time together. He did not put me on the defensive by attempting to prove how much I needed the Lord. Neither did he withhold his witness because of my lack of understanding. He seemed to assume that I was as good as he. In looking back, it is plain to see that he was the bait on the Lord's hook. After the missionary left, without knowing what was happening, I became exceedingly miserable. I did not know that it was the convicting power of the Holy Spirit.

One day in late summer, while riding alone in the car, the fact that I was evading the main issue of life began to dawn on my consciousness. I asked God to make something of my life and there came the sure knowledge that he cared for me and had received me as his own.

Within the next few weeks, a strong desire was placed in my heart to return to college. The thought was to give myself to some form of social service. I wanted to do something to help people. My wife concurred in this and the way opened that Fall of 1947 for me to enrol in a fine Quaker College. Here I was thrown into contact with those Quaker Classics concerned with the inner life and something of prayer as a way of meditation and listening was developed. By the Spring of 1948, there was the strong inner conviction that God wanted me to preach. That Fall I was given an appointment as a student pastor in a Methodist Church in Durham, NC and transferred down to Duke University my senior year.

In becoming a pastor, I felt that I had to prove to the people of this church my worthiness of their acceptance. There was not enough presence of mind or grace of soul to confess to these people my complete inadequacy. Everything became subservient to this role of pastor. Not knowing how to preach, I drew heavily on the published sermons of great preachers. The people liked them and gave me credit for them. I liked their approval. The church began to grow in numbers and interest. We went into a big building programme and there was such total acceptance on every hand that it became easy for me to project myself into the role of the proverbial 'fair-haired boy' who had certain qualities that pertained to the office of bishop.

During my third year as pastor of this church a new dimension of spiritual experience began to be born within me. I had listened much to Rufus Moseley. Contact had been made with others who were spiritually vital. In the midst of what appeared to be a very successful pastorate, a deep spiritual hunger filled my heart. I went from person to person, place to place and church to church seeking fulfilment of what I knew to be a real spiritual need. Many friends thought my only trouble was an attempt to unduly rush my spiritual growth. Ignorance is often expressed in terms of undue caution. I was too hungry to be cautious and kept seeking. Many people were used to help me but none satisfied me. One evening, alone in the church study, I read the words recorded in John 14:15-16 'If ye love me, keep my commandments. And I will pray the Father, and He shall give you another Comforter, that he may abide with you forever.' These words spoke peace to my heart. I did not know Jesus very well and consequently could not lay claim to loving him very much. I certainly could not keep his commandments. I was led to give myself in full consecration to go his way of Love to the extent of my ability. Somehow I knew he would do the rest.

Several weeks passed. One Sunday morning the Sunday School lesson was based on the second chapter of Acts. I attended the adult men's class that morning. Most of the men were members of the official board of the church. When the teacher finished the lesson, he turned to me and asked if I had anything to offer. Something within suggested that I get up in front of all these men whom I served as pastor and tell them about my great need and desire for the experience described in Acts 2. I thought to myself, 'If I tell these men all about my need and searching desire, they will think I am foolish and will lose confidence in me. If this happens, I thought, I'll no longer have a ministry here.' This inward voice seemed to say, 'Well, do you want a ministry or do you want to be baptized with the Holy Ghost?' I got to my feet and came around to the lectern with the full conviction that this meant the end of all my personal desires and dreams in terms of being a successful pastor. I began to make a full confession before these men. I told them how I had feared their opinion, how I had courted their favour and how God had put such a hunger in my heart to be filled with his Spirit. Heaven began to break through. Fear and inhibitions began to depart. Holy Joy and Holy Love began to flood my mind and spirit and body. The high ecstasy continued through the morning worship service. Ignoring my prepared sermon, I came down in front of the chancel and just talked about the Love of Jesus. His Love was being poured out through me in great joy.

Following the service, the entire afternoon was spent in spontaneous praise and thanksgiving. I had prayed before but never like this. Most of my prayer had been petition for self and others or times of meditation and quiet listening. Without an awareness of time, the afternoon was gone and evening service time had come. The evening service was a continuation of the same. After the service, some of the members invited me and others to their home for further prayer. Anytime Jesus gives us anything, he will bring us into contact with someone who will receive it, and usually there is someone to reject it. There were about twenty or thirty people present, most of whom were members of the church which I pastored. I did not know what was happening to me but I was trying to give the loved ones there a description. I was more aware of Heaven than I was of earth and as I sought to describe something of what I saw in the heavenly world, the words were foreign to me. The language being used was not English. Other gifts of the Holy Spirit were made manifest, including the Gift of Knowledge, the Gift of Prophecy, and the Gift of the Discernment of Spirits. The entire world was given new meaning. It even looked different. There is a rare beauty about all God's creation when seen through the eyes of Heaven.

There was such fulfilment of my own desires and needs that it was easy for me to think that everyone needed and wanted the same type of experience. I was prepared to help them and rather free in letting people know it. It was very difficult for many of the members of the church to receive the expression of this experience. Opposition began to mount. The official board took a vote and decided it would be best for the church for me to resign. It seemed pleasing to abide by their decision. Words cannot describe the emotional upheaval that went on within my heart in the face of this rejection. It appeared to be a most tragic experience. Jesus used it to make it one of the greatest experiences of my life. He helped me to see and accept hurt feelings as an expression of pride. He enabled me to see that his Love, like mortar with bricks, not only holds people together but also keeps them properly separated. Without necessarily agreeing with the words used to give description to the experience of the Baptism, our bishop accepted the person who was being baptized. He was most willing to give me another pastoral appointment. He has been and is a helpful friend.

For the next three years, Jesus enabled me to express this New Life in terms of the local church situation. These three years in the pastorate caused me to see that Jesus longs to turn every area of defeat into an area of high victory. Everyone was loving and understanding and God honoured these years with fruitful labour and opened the way for me to receive the appointment of Conference Evangelist.

In the light of my experience and present understanding, I have arrived at the conclusion that the experience of the Baptism of the Holy Spirit is normal Christianity as revealed in the life of the early church. It is not given as an elective course in the school of the Spirit. It is a part of the core curriculum. The promise is to all who hunger and thirst.

chapter three

Cultural Factors

• •

One of the things which has caused a good deal of publicity throughout the second half of 1994 is the prevalence of strange human behaviour during acts of worship in church. The national press has in fact become fascinated with the following kinds of phenomena: drunken behaviour, weeping, laughing, roaring, falling over, shaking, trembling and prophesying. The following report, from the *Daily Express* on Tuesday August 30th, is a typical account of a meeting in which the more characteristic phenomena associated with the Toronto blessing are evident. The reporters are describing a service in a well-known church in London:

> A 10-piece band kicks off the service by thumping out rock-operatic tunes that soon have the congregation waving their arms and jigging in the aisles. During a gentle hymn, a deep laugh rolls out from the gallery; it is picked up around the church. A couple begin to shake, his hands clenching spasmodically, her expression ecstatic. Within minutes the man crouches on the ground. As he slowly keels over to his side, the wife falls backwards into the waiting arms of the Team. After three quarters of an hour they are still prostrate. It turns out they have been 'slain in the Spirit'. The pattern is repeated throughout the congregation. Team members move around, ready for the moment when a worshipper will topple over in a dead faint.

One thing is immediately apparent from this account, namely the amount of physical or bodily reactions to the presence and power of the Holy Spirit. Indeed, later in the report, the writers relate that:

> Normally staid churchgoers are so moved by this force that

they will suddenly cry out, laugh noisily, start speaking in 'tongues' and often weep uncontrollably.

As a consequence of these manifestations, many churches are finding that they are beginning to draw larger numbers than usual. Holy Trinity Brompton, the church about which the *Daily Express* writers were reporting, is a case in point. On the night in question, all 1200 seats for the 6.30 pm service were occupied by 6.10 pm. The queue for the service was being shepherded 45 minutes earlier than that. When one considers that this was an Anglican church, that it was an evening service, and that it was August 30th, this is significant. Most Church of England services on that particular Sunday evening do well to attract 12 people, never mind 1200!

Why is this happening?

It is extremely important for the churches where this apparent 'drunken' behaviour is occurring to appreciate why this kind of thing is taking place, and the low level of significance which the Lord wants us to attribute to it. So why are ecstatic phenomena occurring? How significant are they? In answer to the first question, the reason why they are occurring is simply this: *God always adapts his purposes to the needs of the hour.* Or, put another way, *God always operates in a guise which is appropriate to the culture concerned.* In answer to the second question the ecstatic phenomena attending this present work of the Spirit are the least significant aspect of what God is doing amongst us. They are merely physical and cultural responses to God's power. As such, an emphasis on the manifestations rather than on the deeper intentions of the Lord will almost certainly cause people to miss the real point of what God is doing, which is about empowering the church in order to rescue the lost.

Let me unpack the first of these two answers in detail. I have just written that the Lord operates in a guise which is appropriate to the culture concerned. We can see this quite clearly in the incarnation. When God became a human being in Palestine, he did not choose to appear as a Scandinavian blond, as in so many Sunday School paintings. He became a Jewish boy who grew up into a thoroughly Jewish-looking young adult. That young man did not speak the language of Hollywood but the languages of first-century Palestine – primarily Aramaic, but also probably Hebrew, and a smattering of popular Greek and even Latin. Furthermore, when Jesus began his ministry, he conducted it in a way that was comprehensible to Palestinians of the time. Thus, his style of ministry had aspects of the charismatic *hasid* or holy man, the Jewish rabbi and the wandering Cynic philosopher – all rolled into one! So Jesus the Jew was very much a man of his times and a man for his times. He is the abiding epitome of the principle described above, that *God operates in a guise which is appropriate to the culture concerned*.

The Prevalence of Ecstasy

So what is distinctive about our culture? At this point I need to summarize some of the findings which I have described in my forthcoming book, *Brave New Church*. There my basic proposal is that First-World, Western cultures have evolved into what one may call 'ecstatic or addictive societies'. By that I mean that the contemporary values, fashions, habits, and characteristics of societies like Great Britain promote a lifestyle of ecstatic, mood-altering and escapist activities. These mood-altering activities are basically anaesthetics which blot out the realities of life, and which – however briefly – induce an altered state of consciousness in which our problems disappear. They are 'tranquillizers' which remove pain and which help us – for a little while – to feel good.

In *Brave New Church*, I provide a general overview of the kinds of ecstasy which are currently advertised in the mass media. These are almost invariably forms of addiction. In popular, mainstream culture we first of all see ingestive addictions. These are things which I take into my body (either orally

or intravenously) and which can produce a momentary alter-
ation of my mood, my state of consciousness. The obvious
ones are drugs – both legal, prescription drugs and illicit street
drugs. But chocolate, caffeine, soft drinks of various kinds,
cigarettes, alcohol and a whole host of other ingestive phenomena can induce a temporary 'high' which helps to take the
edge off reality. Even food has this effect on us (unbeknownst
to most people), as the following writer makes plain:

> Each time a person eats, the brain stimulates some of the
> neurochemicals, the endorphins, which are natural painkillers,
> relaxants, and pleasure stimulators. Endorphins are somewhat
> similar to narcotic drugs that produce these results. The
> difference is that they are a natural, God-given part of our
> mechanism, and certain activities stimulate them; such as
> laughter, sexual excitement, eating and aerobic exercise. So,
> after a person has eaten, there is a true state of anaesthesia.

The second category I have defined as 'process addictions'.
These are things which I do as a means of taking a holiday from
reality. Some of the more obvious processes are: sport, parties,
raves, earning money, accumulating possessions, gambling,
violence, perfectionism, success, cleaning, joy-riding (and other
adrenaline addictions), and of course 'shopping'. Any of these,
taken to excess and used as a means of escape, can become
addictive and mood-altering. As far as the last of these is
concerned, shopping, the *Guardian* reported the following
news on Thursday October 6th 1994:

> A study into 'shopping addiction' was launched by
> psychologists yesterday because they believe it can amount to
> a form of illness on a par with compulsive gambling and
> alcoholism. Richard Elliott . . . said yesterday, 'There is a
> syndrome of behaviour involving loss of control over shopping
> and consumption which is very similar to other forms of
> addiction. It is largely, overwhelmingly, seen in women, and it is
> usually carried out in secret' . . . Dr Elliott said it was the

excitement, and the attention from shop assistants, which addictive shoppers craved, not the goods themselves. 'It is a way of coping with depression or anxiety or life problems. It takes their mind off things and gives them a buzz.'

Just about any process can become a means of escape, especially if advertisements push the message that it is possible to attain happiness through them.

A third category of addiction can be described as relational in character. I am referring in particular to the way in which sex and romance can become a means of escaping the pain within. Some people manage to confine their habits to escapist fantasy, enjoying Mills & Boon or romantic films. Others, however, are not so strong. For these people, the 'high' of a sexual conquest, of sexual pleasure, of the feeling of being in love, overpowers them and their lives become unmanageable. Here again, popular mainstream culture conspires to promote passionate sex and intense romance as an easy route to happiness. As Dr Susan Forward has written in her beautifully (though paradoxically) titled book, *Obsessive Love*:

> Popular culture has long cultivated a romantic fascination for obsessive love. In the mini-series 'Napoleon and Josephine' there is a wonderfully erotic scene during which Armand Assante (Napoleon) expresses the power of his love for Jacqueline Bisset (Josephine) by telling her, 'You are my obsession.' A popular perfume uses the same line in its TV ads to promise a shortcut to passion and romance for its users. In the best-selling book *Presumed Innocent* (and in the subsequent movie), the main character still longs for the hot sexuality of his obsessive love affair, even after his lover's death ... Movies, television, advertisements, popular songs – they all collude to persuade us that love is not real unless it is all-consuming.

A fourth category of addiction can be defined as ideological in character. Just about any ideology can become addictive. As a preacher once said, 'All -isms have the power to become addictive and destructive, with the exception of course of baptism and evangelism!' Of particular significance in our contemporary culture is the addictive power of environmentalism. When a genuine and practical care for the planet spills over into a worship of Gaia or 'mother earth', when eco-sensitivity evolves into eco-idolatry, then the pursuit of ecstasy is not far away. Indeed, some of the more primitive and tribal practices of the emerging neo-paganism (such as Sun-worship) amply demonstrate the deep urge for self-transcendence in many people. Thus we see the addictive power of -isms in our culture. Nationalism, militarism, fascism, racism, communism, vegetarianism, patriotism – just about any ISM – can become a means of self-transcendence, in short, a means of ecstasy.

A final category of addiction is 'technological' in character. In contemporary, mainstream culture we cannot avoid the present technolatry, the present idolatry of technology, promoted by the mass media. Indeed, a whole generation of techno-junkies is growing up all around us – children and young people who have learnt to escape into the artificial paradises marketed by Sega and Nintendo, and now increasingly by much more sophisticated forms of consumer electronics such as Virtual Reality. A generation is evolving in our day which has learnt the art of becoming 'comfortably numb' through TV (widescreen, Dolby surround), Interactive CD-Rom, Hi-Fi, Video, Laser, Cinema, Computer Games, the Internet and so on. Indeed, on September 22nd 1994, the *Daily Express* reporter Robert McGowan stressed this same point in an article entitled 'Joystick Junkies', subtitled, 'Children crave video games like heroin addicts need a fix'. McGowan's piece was mainly about computer games, the biggest leisure phenomenon in recent years. He quotes a lecturer from Plymouth University:

> The addiction to these games is comparable to addiction to alcohol, gambling, nicotine and heroin.

But his warning is applicable to other technological phenomena in our Cyber-oriented culture.

The Power of Ecstasy

My point in *Brave New Church* is a simple and obvious one: we are fast becoming a society which gets high on ingestive, process, relational, ideological and technological phenomena. We are becoming an ecstatic, addictive, 'quick-fix' society. Nothing symbolizes this truth more poignantly than the drug popularly called 'Ecstasy'. In a recent Equinox programme on Channel 4 called 'Rave New World', the point was made that hundreds of thousands of people today are pursuing happiness, and finding it in a techno trip comprising technology, dance, music and drugs. This heady mixture has created a rave culture in which Ecstasy has become a key stimulant. At airport hangars, clubs and warehouses, young people come and dance all night to a music with virtually no lyrics, and whose repetitive rhythms pound the ears with up to 180 beats per minute. At least some of these young people take Ecstasy, a drug taken in pill form which induces in many people a state of euphoria by forcing the neurons in the brain to release large quantities of serotonin. This, along with the recent use of psychedelic graphics, combines with the effect of the music to create the following kinds of response, cited in the Channel 4 programme:

> There was just this massive rush of, to me, happiness, because there was a genuine brilliant atmosphere in the club and everybody was basically feeding off each other.

> All of a sudden I got this huge *whoosh* running through my body and out of it, sort of thing – don't know where it went – a huge energy force almost.

> And this would just build up and the whole crowd would just be like going along with it and becoming more and more frantic until you did actually feel as if you were slightly losing control.

It hits you and it bombards you and it breaks down any of those barriers between us. The rhythm just grabs hold of you.

I actually came away from that thinking: I have just had the best night of my life, and I really thought I have never had a better time. It was just the happiest.

I thought it was much better than the sex I'd had because it was just so much happier, it was with just so many people and it was such a good shared experience that made it much more powerful.

These quotations make plain 'the power of ecstasy' – both Ecstasy the drug, and ecstasy the state of mind. They reveal a brave new world of people desperate for community, for happiness, for thrills. The problem is, of course, that most look for it in the wrong places. Raves do not provide community. The kinds of groups established at raves are momentary, fluid tribes, not stable, committed, ongoing communities. Furthermore, the kind of happiness achieved in such gatherings is only temporary; it does not sustain the subject through the working week, nor through the problems of the real world – which return as surely as the dawn. Everything about this experience in fact exacts a price. Ecstasy, for example, can kill. The effects of dehydration on dancers can be (and has been) fatal. A sexual partner who has felt so good and so right the night before has turned out, in the cool light of day, to be the most unsuitable companion. Thus, in the final analysis, the rave culture is perhaps the most vivid and graphic example of the widespread quest for ecstasy in society today.

The Irrelevant Church

In a culture like this, a very legitimate question might be, 'What has the church got which might offer a viable and positive alternative to all this ecstasy?' At this point I would like to make reference to what I consider to be one of the most helpful articles ever written on this subject, Dr Howard Clinebell's 'Philosophical-Religious Factors in the Etiology and Treatment of Alcoholism'. This article is specifically about 'highs' induced by alcohol, but it is extremely relevant to the broader discussion already underway in this chapter.

Clinebell begins by proposing that the ecstasy induced by alcohol is in fact an attempt by the drinker to find God in a bottle (Bill Wilson's phrase). Clinebell quotes William James' comment, in *The Varieties of Religious Experience*, that 'the sway of alcohol over mankind is unquestionably due to its power to stimulate the mystical faculties of human nature'. He goes on to suggest that people who drink alcohol to excess are often striving for a pseudo-mystical experience, and he offers an explanation why:

> When ancient man stumbled by accident on the product of fermentation, he must have felt that strange, even miraculous, things were happening to his inner world. When he drank the juice of fruit, grains or honey which had been left in a warm place for a time, his fears and burdens lost their weight. His painful awareness of disease, death and injustice lost its sting. The monotony and drabness of his life were interrupted. He felt lifted out of the horizontal earth-boundness of his daily existence into a temporary experience of the vertical dimension of life. Small wonder that he regarded the substance that could produce these effects as a mysterious gift of the gods.

Clinebell proceeds to demonstrate how alcohol was used in ancient religions, such as the worship of the Greek god Dionysus, because of its power to give experiences of the ecstatic and the transcendent. Clinebell, in other words, underscores the intimate connection between religion and alcohol in the ancient world. He also underscores its connection in the modern world. Indeed, he proposes that drinking alcohol in order to get drunk is in fact an attempt to satisfy religious needs by non-religious means – i.e. by alcoholic intoxication. The essential problems which the drinker is seeking to mask through alcohol are, Clinebell argues, religious or spiritual in character. He proposes that there are three fundamental needs in each one of us, and that these are spiritual not just psychological:

1 The need to experience the numinous, the transcendent.

2 The need for a sense of meaning, purpose and value in one's life.

3 The need for a feeling of deep trust and relatedness to life.

At the root of these three needs is what Clinebell calls, 'existential anxiety' – the anxiety induced by a human being's sense of his mortality, of the fact that he must die.

Clinebell then argues that 'There is no psychological answer to existential anxiety. It cannot be eliminated through psychotherapy.' There are only pseudo-religious or genuinely religious ways of dealing with it. Pseudo-religious means involve drinking alcohol to excess, or taking Ecstasy, or indulging in an obsessive way in any of the ingestive, process, relational, ideological or technological addictions mentioned earlier. These offer a temporary unitive and ecstatic experience, but when the magic moments pass, the user finds that the gulf is wider and the isolation deeper than ever before. What, then, is the alternative? Genuine religious answers should, in Clinebell's opinion, come from the church. There is a problem, however:

> We live in a period of history when it is not easy to find genuinely religious answers. Contemporary religion in the West has lost much of the sense of the numinous and the transcendent ... Many contemporary religious expressions are pale and anemic, lacking in the ecstatic, the mystical, the numinous. When religion loses its spine-tingling quality, alcohol is substituted by many.

The problem, then, is that the church has become irrelevant in an ecstatic culture. It stubbornly sustains a rationalistic, formalistic and abstract form, when the culture it is supposed to be serving is crying out for the opposite: the experiential, the spontaneous and the immanent.

The Divine Alternative

At this point we must turn to Scripture for, as always, the wisdom we need to guide us through the present uncertainties of our changing culture are to be found in its timeless truths. The key passage in this present context is Ephesians 5:15–20, where Paul (I do take the author to be Paul) offers the following counsel:

> Be very careful, then, how you live – not as unwise but as wise, making the most of every opportunity, because the days are evil. Therefore, do not be foolish, but understand what the Lord's will is. Do not get drunk on wine, which leads to debauchery. Instead, be filled with the Spirit. Speak to one another with psalms, hymns and spiritual songs. Sing and make music in your hearts to the Lord, always giving thanks to God the Father for everything, in the name of our Lord Jesus Christ.

In this passage, Paul is addressing Christians not non-Christians. He explains to them (and by extension to us) that Christians are consistently presented with lifestyle choices. He articulates three of these in the form of a 'not . . . but' (*me . . . alla*) construction:

not unwise, but wise

not foolish, but understanding

not intoxicated by wine, but filled with the Spirit.

The last of these is the most relevant to our present discussion, though ultimately all three are linked. Paul says, 'Do not get drunk on wine, which leads to debauchery, but be filled with the Spirit.' Here the stark choice is presented in the form of an imperative, in the form of a command. We have a choice between two lifestyles, and the Word of God commands us to make the right choice. The two options available to us are 'getting drunk on wine, which leads to debauchery', or 'being filled with the Spirit'. As is often pointed out, the imperative 'be filled' is in fact a present continuous: 'Go on being filled with the Spirit'. Paul exhorts us to choose this way of life – a life of consistent charismatic fullness – rather than a life of wine-bibbing.

What kind of situation in the Ephesian church made these words of Paul so important? In a recent article entitled 'The Dionysian Background of Ephesians 5:18', Cleon Rogers takes up a point made by Marcus Barth that Paul presents the choice between alcoholic intoxication and pneumatic fullness because Ephesus was a hot-bed of Dionysian behaviour at the time. Rogers argues that:

> The wild, drunken practices connected with the worship of Dionysus or Bacchus, the god of wine, form the general cultural background for Paul's two commands in Ephesians 5:18.

The cult of Dionysus, Rogers argues, was widespread in the ancient world. Though the worship of Artemis (Diana) was the primary cult in Ephesus, it is clear from the historical evidence that that of Dionysus was well established there, as it was in practically every major city which Paul visited. Thus Rogers cites Plutarch's description of what occurred when Anthony entered the city of Ephesus:

> Women arrayed like Bacchanals, and men and boys like Satyrs and Pans, led the way before him and the city was full of ivy and thyrus wands and harps and pipes and flutes, the people hailing him as Dionysus, giver of Joy . . .
> (*Lives, Antony* 24:3).

At the heart of Dionysian worship there were a number of constants. First of all, there was a frequent emphasis upon fertility and sex. Secondly, there was always wild, frenzied dancing, involving the music of flutes, cymbals, drums, or tambourines. Thirdly, women (the maenads) took a prominent role, dancing in the mountains and often – in a frenzied state – eating the raw flesh of animals. Fourthly, the drinking of wine was common. The purpose of this intoxication was to have the god Dionysus possess you with 'enthusiasm'. Fifthly, unusual phenomena occurred in the woods where these activities took place. Dionysus was said to have appeared in the form of various animals. Milk, honey and wine were also seen bubbling out of the ground. All in all, then, Dionysian ecstasy was both dramatic in character and widespread in appeal. Those who took part experienced a cathartic release from the stresses of everyday life. 'It was especially the women', Rogers writes, 'who felt lifted above their lowly status in life and felt freed from the weary burden of their work.'

Rogers proposes that Christians in Ephesus wanted to have their cake and eat it. They wanted what we would now call an addictive lifestyle and at the same time they wanted to be Christians. Confronted by this flagrant example of compromise, Paul says that believers are not to get drunk on wine but to go on being filled with the Spirit. He commands them not to mix their spirits but to have their lives filled with the one Spirit, the Holy Spirit of God. They were not to run after worldly and demonic counterfeits of Christian ecstasy. Filling one's body with the spirit of Dionysus (through wine) would merely lead to a terminal state of 'debauchery' or 'excess' (a better translation of *asotia*). Instead, they were to go on being filled with the supernatural Spirit of the Living God. Only then could they enjoy the wholesome, Christian alternative to Dionysian inebriation – an alternative in which they could worship with psalms, hymns and spiritual songs (as opposed to frenzied dancing); in which they could sing and make music in their hearts to the Lord (not to Dionysus); in which they could enjoy the true, God-given order for domestic relationships (Ephesians 5:22–6:4), rather than the wild disorder of the Dionysian cult. Being filled with the Holy Spirit, in short, is Paul's divine alternative.

Charismatic Intoxication

This last point needs stressing. Behind Paul's reasoning in this passage lies the knowledge that being filled with the Holy Spirit is a felt experience which often results in ecstatic joy. In fact, it is fairly certain that Paul is contrasting two forms of intoxication – one involving wine, the other involving the Holy Spirit. This was, after all, a fairly common contrast. Philo, for example, wrote:

> Now when grace fills the soul, that soul thereby rejoices and smiles and dances, for it is possessed and inspired, so that to many of the unenlightened it may seem to be drunken, crazy, and beside itself . . . For with the God-possessed not only is the soul wont to be stirred and goaded as it were into ecstasy, but the body is flushed and fiery . . . and thus many of the foolish are deceived and suppose that the sober are drunk . . . and it is true that these sober ones are drunk in a sense (De Ebr, 146–8).

Luke makes a similar contrast to this in his description of the Pentecost event. When the Holy Spirit fell upon the disciples and filled all of them, they were certainly moved to behave with what looked at the very least like enthusiasm, and perhaps to some like abandonment. Indeed, some cynics standing by accused them of actually being drunk – something which Peter felt led to refute by saying that it was only nine o'clock in the morning. Clearly, the disciples looked intoxicated when they declared the wonders of the Lord in unlearnt foreign languages. As such, their behaviour was mistaken by some for the kind of cultic inebriation associated with Dionysus.

All this, of course, is extremely relevant to the present chapter. The truth of the matter is this: when a society becomes addictive and ecstatic, people seek to take holidays from reality by resorting to ingestive, process, relational, ideological or technological pleasures. In Paul's more simple terminology, they seek to get drunk on wine which leads to excess. However, the church is God's radical counter-culture. Here the Lord provides, as it were, a redemptive alternative to the ecstatic experiences offered by the world. His alternative is the dynamic experience of being filled with the Spirit. This Spirit is not any old 'spirit'. He is the Spirit who enables us to give thanks to the Father in the name of

the Son (Ephesians 5:20). This Spirit is emphatically the Holy
Spirit. He is the third person of the Divine Trinity. As a consequence, being filled, controlled and possessed by this Spirit is not
a dangerous experience, leading to sexual promiscuity, inebriation and frenzied dancing (as was the case in the Dionysiac fren-
zies). The Spirit of God is altogether holy, altogether Christ-like,
altogether trustworthy. To be possessed by this Spirit is to be
possessed by something far better, far more wholesome, than
anything the world has on offer.

We find this particularly true during times of revival. In the
Welsh Revival earlier this century, R. B. Jones comments as
follows:

> The effect on the drink-habit of many was very striking. The
> public-houses, almost at a stroke, became practically empty.
> Brewery concerns found, in this movement of the Spirit of
> God, something that seriously affected their dividends.
> Publicans were badly hit, and openly confessed the
> tremendous diminution in their takings. Bankruptcy overtook
> some, but, better still, some of them were converted and
> surrendered their licenses. In one place a public-house was
> turned into a house of prayer, so was a drinking-club, in
> another district. Even men who were not converts were
> ashamed to be seen entering such places.

Clearly, being filled with the Holy Spirit was preferable to
being filled with alcohol. The joy of knowing God the Father,
through Jesus Christ, and in the power of the Holy Spirit, far
surpassed any other pleasure on offer in Wales at the time. The
high ecstasy of knowing the pardon of Calvary and the power
of Pentecost outdid any other experience. It does today.

The Needs of the Culture

Returning to the point made earlier, God always operates in a
guise which is appropriate to the culture. Since ours is a largely

Dionysian culture – a culture of addicts looking for ecstasy – God has chosen to operate during this time of refreshing by permitting many ecstatic phenomena – such as shaking, fainting, falling over, weeping, laughing, roaring, and generally drunken behaviour. All of this looks to outsiders just like Dionysian abandonment. It feels to cynical observers like possession, inebriation, loss of control and so on. But in a Dionysian culture, God graciously respects the needs of the hour. Since one of the deep needs of many people is the need for ecstasy, the Lord allows us to experience the uninhibited joy of knowing Jesus Christ in a number of varied, ecstatic ways – including some which look very strange. To those who object to this, three things need to be said. First, we cannot dictate to God how he is to act in a particular situation. The Holy Spirit determines how he is to manifest himself in us (I Corinthians 12:8–11). Secondly, there is any case something genuinely ecstatic about knowing Jesus Christ. Anyone who has experienced the heady delight of being indwelt by Jesus Christ in the power of the Spirit knows that! Thirdly, there are historical precedents for what is happening now. Revivals in addictive societies have usually involved a high degree of ecstatic phenomena.

This third point is worth elaborating. If we look at the socio-economic character of England prior to the revival involving John and Charles Wesley (as well as George Whitefield and many others), one thing can definitely be said about it: it was an addictive society, as ours is today. English society then was where the consumer culture was born. It was also marked by the particularly grave evil of alcoholism. At the start of the eighteenth century, the popular alcoholic drink was beer or ale. The consumption of beer was astonishing. In 1688, there was an estimated population of 5,000,000 in England, and during that year a staggering 12,400,000 barrels were brewed. In 1724, however, a new evil appeared on the scene – the habit of gin-drinking. This spread with the rapidity of an epidemic throughout the whole population. The statistics reveal the alarming rate at which the whole country quickly caught the craze. In 1684, 527,000 gallons of spirits were distilled. In

1714, 2,000,000 were distilled. In 1727, that rose to 3,601,000, in 1735 to 5,394,000 and in 1742 to more than 7,000,000 gallons. Between 1750 and 1751, over 11,000,000 gallons of spirits were consumed.

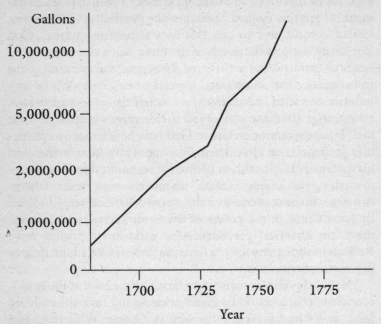

Indeed, as is well known, retailers of gin used to announce that customers could be made drunk for a penny, dead-drunk for two pence, and could have straw to lie on in the cellar for nothing. The popularity of this kind of drunken anaesthesia can be gauged by the fact that the number of gin shops numbered more than 17,000 in 1749. Drunkenness, in fact, became something respectable. Thus the tombstone of Rebecca Freeland (who died in 1741) read:

> She drank good ale, good punch, and wine
> And lived to the age of ninety-nine.

There was therefore something wildly Dionysian about this

supposedly idyllic, Georgian Age. Indeed, a love of violence (so characteristic of Dionysian worship) took root in society during the first half of the eighteenth century. Fielding wrote a pamphlet in 1751 entitled, 'On the late Increase in Robbers' which highlighted the new craze of street violence, particularly gang muggings. At the beginning of the century, London's streets were plagued by a club of upper-class young men called 'the Mohocks', whose favourite pastime was something called 'tipping the lion' – a particularly brutal act involving squeezing the nose of their victim flat upon his face, and then boring out his eyes with their fingers. Other similar groups formed, assuming glamorous names such as 'sweaters', 'tumblers', and the 'dancing masters'. Other acts of violence became an addiction. Sailors at sea were lured by false signals to the rocks and then plundered. Public hangings became a spectacle of entertainment, with condemned felons more determined to die in style than to escape their fate. On one famous occasion in 1735, a man who had murdered his wife was sentenced to be hanged but chose to poison himself instead. Angry at having been cheated of the spectacle, the crowd exhumed his body and, as the *Gentleman's Magazine* put it, 'dragged his guts about the highway, poked his eyes out, and broke almost all his bones'.

Such was the addictive nature of the eighteenth-century society. Britain became, in the words of one writer, a 'dizzy island'. This dizziness was everywhere visible. Eminent politicians were renowned for being 'drunk as lords'. Robert Walpole's household, during one year (1733), consumed over 1,000 bottles of White Lisbon wine alone. Handsome eating became a token of success, with Englishmen taking great pride in their enormous bellies. Thus Dr Samuel Johnson could declare without shame:

> I mind my belly very well, for I look upon it that he who will not mind his belly will scarcely mind anything else.

Gambling became another source of anaesthesia. Bets were laid on just about anything. Indeed, you could get four to one on George II being killed in the war against the French in 1743. Cards were very popular, and a state lottery was run from 1709 to 1824 – with various institutions like the British Museum being partially supported by the proceeds. There was also an inevitable deterioration in sexual morality. As Roy Porter puts it, 'The libido was liberated, and erotic gratification increasingly dissociated from sin and shame'. Lewd songs were popular, erotic literature multiplied unchecked, the newspapers were full of advertisements for various sexual services – Georgian frankness was, in short, 'unmatched'.

The squalor and unpleasantness of life became tolerated as a result of the relentless pursuit of pleasure. Life's pains were forgotten in a great orgy of hedonism. What mattered to most was the unbridled pursuit of happiness in the here-and-now. Thus Soame Jenyns could write:

> Happiness is the only thing of real value in existence: neither riches, nor power, nor wisdom, nor learning, nor strength, nor beauty, nor virtue, nor religion, nor even life itself, being of any importance but as they contribute to its production.

So Britain in the first half of the eighteenth century became a nation high on every kind of addiction – a fact which Hogarth captured so poignantly in his picture of Gin Lane. Britain was a nation gripped by the need to forget the harsh realities of life through any means possible. Violence, gambling, alcohol, sex, anything – even coffee (for this was the age of the coffee shop) was used as a means of escape. Perhaps no incident more clearly demonstrates the numbness of the times than this one, recorded in the *Gentleman's Magazine* in 1748:

> At a Christening at Beddington in Surrey the nurse was so intoxicated that after she had undressed the child, instead of laying it in the cradle she put it behind a large fire, which burnt it to death in a few minutes. She was examined before a magistrate, and said she was quite stupid and senseless, so that she took the child for a log of wood; on which she was discharged.

The World in the Church

One of the reasons why eighteenth-century Britain deterio-
rated so dramatically was because the Church (principally the
Anglican Church) was not offering a radical alternative to the
culture. Roy Porter makes the point that

> Many Georgians rarely went through a church porch between
> their christening and burial. Yet practically everyone, in his
> own fashion, had faith. Much of it was a fig leaf of Christianity
> covering a body of inherited magic and superstition.

Joseph Addison complained that 'There is less appearance of
religion in England than in any neighbouring state.' Churches
were being closed down at an alarming late. In London there
were seventy-two churches which offered daily services in 1714.
By 1732 that had dwindled to forty-four. About a quarter of
the Anglican parishes in England at this time did not have an
incumbent resident within the parish. Indeed, by 1780, 70% of
the rectors in Devon were non-resident. The Church (particularly the Anglican Church) was therefore dying.

Why, then, were people not going to church? Why was
private faith preferred to public worship? The answer to that
is because the Church of England was too infected by the
spirit of the age to provide a magnetic counter-culture.
Theologically, many clergy had bought into the rationalistic
and mechanistic view known as Deism. Deists proposed
(putting it very simplistically) that God was like a watch-
maker, the world was like a watch, and that God stood outside
his creation, which ran like clockwork on its own. Thus, in
terms of theology, the prevailing opinion stressed the tran-
scendence rather than the immanence of God. There was little
sense of the nearness, the reality and the presence of God,
except amongst the Enthusiasts. But then the Bishop of
Durham (Joseph Butler) said of enthusiasm that it was 'a most
horrid thing'.

Furthermore, many clergy (including bishops) preached

tolerance in the face of consumerism, pluralism and hedonism. Thus Voltaire observed:

> Enter the London stock exchange . . . You will see the deputies of all nations gathered there for the service of mankind. There a Jew, a Mohammedan, and the Christian deal with each other as if they were of the same religion . . . On leaving these free and peaceful assemblies, some go to the synagogue, others to drink; this one goes to have himself baptized in the name of the Father, the Son, and the Holy Ghost; that one has his son's foreskin cut off and Hebrew words mumbled over the child which he does not understand; others go to church to await the inspiration of God, their hats on their heads; and all are content.

No wonder John Wesley described the age as follows:

> Ungodliness is our universal, our constant, our peculiar character . . . a total ignorance of God is almost universal among us – High and low, cobblers, tinkers, hackney coachmen, men and maid servants, soldiers, tradesmen of all rank, lawyers, physicians, gentlemen, lords are as ignorant of the Creator of the World as Mohametans and Pagans.

The singular failure of the Anglican Church in the eighteenth century therefore has to be honestly confessed. There was far too much of the world in the church and not nearly enough of the church in the world. Both the unchurched society and those who went to church were guilty of wanting 'a basically secular life with the comforts of religion superadded'. As such, the churches were not full. They were not places where an addict might find, in Sarah Edwards' beautiful words, a sense of 'my dearness to God, and his nearness to me'. There were places devoid of what Clinebell called the numinous, spine-tingling sense of God's presence. As a consequence, society sought to fulfil religious needs through pseudo-religious means.

A Brave New Church
• • • • • • • • • • • • • • • • • • • •

It was in this situation that God raised up men like the two Wesleys and George Whitefield. Whilst the Church of England continued to decline, a new Church was born out of the courageous Gospel-preaching of men like John Wesley. Whitefield and both Wesleys preached saving faith – in other words, that we are saved by faith in Christ, and by that alone. Many churches were closed to them, but some opened their doors with remarkable results. Thus Whitefield recorded the following in his journal:

> I had an opportunity of preaching in the morning at St Helen's, and at Islington in the afternoon, to large congregations indeed, with great demonstrations of the Spirit, and with great power. Here seems to be a great pouring out of the Spirit, and many who were awakened by my preaching a year ago, are now grown strong men in Christ, by the ministrations of my dear friends and fellow-labourers, John and Charles Wesley.

What these men provided, then, was something utterly different from what most of the clergy of the day were offering. They first of all preached the Good News; in other words, that we are dreadful sinners in the sight of God, but that God has given us a means of forgiveness and reconciliation through the atoning death of his Son, Jesus Christ. This, then, was no rationalistic theology. This was a Bible theology which could be readily understood by the poor and uneducated – by those largely neglected by the churches. Secondly, they were men who were open to what Whitefield, citing I Corinthians 2:4, calls 'demonstrations of the Spirit, with great power'. In fact, these were men who knew the power and the pattern of Pentecost. The well-known words of John Wesley (concerning an all-night prayer meeting on January 1st 1739) bear this out:

> About three in the morning, as we were continuing instant in prayer, the power of God came mightily upon us, insomuch

that many cried out for exceeding joy, and many fell to the
ground. As soon as we were recovered a little from that awe
and amazement at the presence of his majesty, we broke out
with one voice, 'We praise thee, O God; we acknowledge
thee to be the Lord!'

Thirdly, these men sought to provide a lifestyle of holy absti-
nence in a culture gripped by a stronghold of hedonism. The
Evangelical movement, particularly in the second half of the
eighteenth century, sought to purge all signs of addiction from
their spirituality. Thus the *Evangelical Magazine* published the
following Spiritual Barometer in 1800:

70 —	Glory: dismission from the body.
60 —	Desiring to depart to be with Christ; patience in tribulation; glorying in the cross.
50 —	Ardent love to the souls of men; followed hard after God: Deadness to the world by the cross of Christ.
40 —	Love of God, shed abroad in the heart; frequent approach to the Lord's Table; meeting for prayer and experience.
30 —	Delight in the people of God; looking to Jesus.
20 —	Love of God's house and word; daily perusal of the Bible with prayer; vain company wholly dropped.
10 —	Evangelical light; retirement for prayer and meditation; concern for the soul; alarm.
0 —	Indifference; family worship only on Sunday evenings; private prayer frequently omitted; family religion wholly declined.
10 —	Levity in conversations; fashions, however expensive or indecent, adopted.
20 —	Luxurious entertainment; free association with carnal company.
30 —	The theatre; Vauxhall; Ranelagh, etc.; frequent parties of pleasure; home of God forsaken; much wine, spirits, etc.
40 —	Love of novels, etc.; scepticism; private prayer totally neglected; deistical company prized.
50 —	Parties of pleasure on the Lord's day; masquerades; drunkenness; adultery; profaneness; lewd songs.
60 —	Infidelity; jesting at religion; sitting down in the chair of the scoffer.
70 —	Death; perdition.

This demonstrates how the Evangelical Revival attempted to lead people into what I call 'decaffeinated discipleship' (a lifestyle with all addictive elements removed) in the midst of a hedonistic society.

The result of this tremendous revival was that a brave new Church was born. Originally it had not been Wesley's intention to begin a new denomination. His desire was for a renewed Anglicanism. However, that vision did not materialize and the movement known as Methodism was born. This movement grew as the end of the century drew closer. In 1767 there were 24,000 Methodists. By 1796 there were 77,000. This movement was a movement of the Holy Spirit of enormous significance. Many historians, indeed, have suggested that a Revolution as bloody as that which crippled France between 1789–93 was averted in England because of the way in which the Evangelical revival generated a lasting self-respect among converts. As Roy Porter puts it, in arguably one of the best historical overviews of English society in the eighteenth century:

> What first galvanized large sections of the work-force into self-help and self-respect were not polite letters, Enlightenment rationalism or Deism, but Methodism and New Dissent. And when polite society itself felt the earthquake tremors of revolution at the close of the century, it was to religious . . . revival – to God – that it turned.

Parallels with Society Today

There are so many echoes between English society in the 1740s and English society in the 1990s that the dictum 'history repeats itself' seems frighteningly true. Both English society then and English society now can be described as Dionysian and addictive in character. The same pursuit of pleasure through all means possible, the same desire to fill the hole in the soul through pseudo-religious things, the same desperate urge to transcend present ills through ecstasy, are plainly visible in both contexts. What is also clearly present in both societies is a weak and ineffective Church. Both the Anglican Church in the eighteenth century, and the Anglican Church in the twentieth century, have failed to make their mark. Both show signs of contamination by Enlightenment rationalism and cultural hedonism. Neither has succeeded in bringing a dizzy nation into a sense of the nearness of the Father, the forgiveness of the Son, and the new life lived in the power of the Holy Spirit. When Roy Porter says, 'The year 1800 dawned with the Anglican Church ill-equipped to serve the nation', many of us will feel that the same may one day be said of the year 2000.

The news, however, is not all 'doom and gloom'. As I wrote at the start of this chapter, the Lord always adapts his ministry to the needs of the hour. He always operates in a guise which is appropriate to the culture. In eighteenth-century England, where people were seeking after happiness in all the wrong places, that meant a high level of ecstatic phenomena in many church meetings. It meant presenting the nation with the divine alternative: being filled with the Holy Spirit rather than with an alcoholic spirit. When John Wesley and others preached the Gospel, they consequently found that people were often led into the high ecstasies of the Spirit. Thus Wesley records of his preaching at Newgate Prison in Bristol:

> One, and another, and another sunk to the earth: they dropped on every side as thunderstruck. One of them cried aloud. We besought God on her behalf and he turned her heaviness into joy. A second being in the same agony, we called upon God for her also; and he spoke peace unto her soul.

As the century draws to a close in our own times, we see a similar work occurring in our own society. We too have become an ecstatic, addictive society. We too are looking for God in a bottle, as it were. It is therefore no coincidence that the Toronto blessing is being attended by a large number of ecstatic phenomena – falling down, shaking, laughing, trembling, shouting out, roaring and (especially significant) drunken behaviour. In many respects this is entirely predictable. For those whose religious affections have been suppressed, the present work of the Spirit has brought a great release of emotion. For those whose Christianity has been dominated by a rationalistic, formalistic religiosity, this blessing has brought a fresh sense of the reality, the nearness and the intimacy of God in actual experience. For those who have been living an addictive lifestyle, this intoxicating infusion of God's Holy Spirit has produced a true awakening concerning where solid joys and lasting pleasures are really to be found. This is, in short, the way the Lord chooses to operate when society becomes an addict.

As a brief example of this, take the following extract from a letter which was sent to me on my arrival as vicar of St Mark's Church, Grenoside, here in Sheffield:

> The main reason for writing is to invite you to a wine tasting evening here on Saturday the 25th September. I don't know if you have heard of the Wine Club. It is a somewhat riotous occasion and I should warn you that you may see some of your parishioners in a slightly different light! However, if you wish to take the risk, you would be most welcome. We normally start at about 8.00 pm . . . Please don't worry about driving home afterwards as we hope to provide transport to save anyone having to stagger up the hill. I hope you can come. I know Sunday is a big day . . . and we would ensure you were not too late getting home. The food and wine are usually finished by about 11.00 pm but folks usually stay a little after that. It varies.

Immediately I received this letter my heart sank. I had heard about these occasions from the previous vicar, and I had been greatly displeased to hear that some of the worst offenders at these events were regular attenders at church. I therefore declined the invitation.

Several months later, however, the couple who had sent the

letter started to experience severe difficulties. Over the course of several weeks support and prayer it became clear that there was a hunger in their hearts to rededicate themselves to Christ and to be filled with the Holy Spirit. Three of us duly visited them and prayed for them with the laying on of hands. Afterwards, the same woman who had written the original letter wrote the following:

> I felt that I must write and thank you for your helpful ministry to us on Tuesday. We are still basking in the afterglow! I shall never forget the experience of God's power and the way you worked together in such harmony to allow it to happen. Since then I have felt cleansed through my whole being and also great joy, in spite of our present difficult circumstances. Only the Lord could do this, for which I give him thanks and praise!

That was in October 1993. Today, one year later, this couple have gone from being at the fringe of the church to being at the very centre. They both work tremendously hard for the Lord. Though their circumstances have not changed much financially, their lifestyle has changed radically. They are truly holy, committed, Spirit-filled people who have found that being filled with the Holy Spirit is far, far better than getting drunk on wine.

Some Pitfalls

In this chapter I have suggested that the Lord operates in a guise which is appropriate to the culture. Ours is an addictive culture – a culture of people looking for ecstasy in some very unwise places. As a consequence, the present work of the Holy Spirit is involving a very high level of ecstatic phenomena. This is, I believe, God's way of attracting the attention of many people today, especially those in the youth sub-cultures, and those belonging to the baby-boom generation. These group-ings find the festal, ecstatic nature of church meetings very attractive, which is why there are queues at places like Holy Trinity Brompton. Such people are turned on by the party spirit. Older people, by and large, find these ecstatic phenomena more disturbing and off-putting. They have learnt from a savage world war that suffering is part of life; suffering is something to be borne with a stiff upper lip – with dignity and without complaint. This portion of the population is not composed, by and large, of people who resort to ingestive, process, relational, ideological and technological addiction in order to mask the pain. The older generation is not seeking after ecstatic experiences in the way many teenagers and twenty/thirty-somethings are. Ecstatic phenomena in church therefore have far less appeal for them.

What this clearly demonstrates is the fact that the present manifestations (such as drunken behaviour) are only the cultural packaging of the work of the Spirit. They are the wrapping, not the gift itself. They are the form, not the content of what God wants to do. As a result, we must answer the second question posed at the start of this chapter with honesty and realism. That question concerned how much significance we should attach to the ecstatic phenomena which are visible in many services and meetings. The right response to that is to say that the phenomena are insignificant. They are, in a sense, the least important facet of what God is doing. They are the froth on the wave, as we shall see in the context of ecstatic laughter in the next chapter. They are the physical and cultural reactions to the powerful presence and work of the Holy Spirit. To say otherwise, and thereby give them undue importance, will lead us up a very dangerous path. That path has a number of pitfalls.

1. The pitfall of manifestation without declaration

I see a real danger at the moment of divorcing the gifts from the Gospel. In other words, there is a danger of preaching about manifestations of the Spirit, and then praying 'Come, Holy Spirit!' directly afterwards. This, however, runs the dreadful risk of manipulation through a process of suggestion. We need to learn from previous revivals here. When we read the accounts of Whitefield, John Wesley and Charles Wesley, (as well as Jonathan Edwards and others) it is abundantly clear that dramatic manifestations of the Spirit occurred during and after the preaching of the Gospel. Manifestation, in other words, accompanied declaration – the declaration of the sin of man and the grace of God. As in the Acts of the Apostles, this was a case of the Gospel and the gifts going together. The preaching of the Word was attended by signs following. What these men never did was preach about laughter, shaking, fainting and other phenomena. They declared the wonderful truths of the Gospel. We must be sure to do the same.

2. The pitfall of manifestation without transformation

In an addictive society like ours, there is always a danger of charismatic grabbitism – of people going to meetings again and again in order to get high on the experience of the Spirit. Rev. Philip Smith, whom I have referred to already, makes an interesting point about the difference between the import-ance of ecstatic experience at the beginning of the Charismatic renewal (1960s) and its importance today. In a letter he wrote these words to me:

> One thing which needs to be emphasized is that in those early days, those few of us in the mainline churches whom the Lord was targeting did not seek any emotional experiences or external thrills or 'spiritual fireworks'. In fact, most of us feared mere emotionalism or outward display, and we didn't really want 'speaking in tongues', but understood that this was part of the Divine 'package deal'. And as we studied unfamiliar territory in the Scriptures regarding tongues, we had to admit that glossolalia seemed to be an important part of accepting the working of the Holy Spirit in the Christian's life . . . I would see here a real contrast with the 'Toronto Blessing' and the expectations particularly of young Christians. In a secular culture that has become used to 'getting high' on drugs etc., there is a danger that Christians will start to expect and clamour for outward manifestations and external phenomena.

Those are wise words of warning. In our present scene there is a danger of people becoming addicted to ecstatic experiences of the Holy Spirit. In such a time as this, the Lord's word seems to be 'manifestation without transformation is worthless'. In other words, what matters is not the superficial phenomena (the physical, psychological and cultural reactions to the Spirit's power upon us) but the deeper work which the Lord is doing in us. That deeper work is primarily about repentance, about holiness, about equipping for mission, and so forth. It is upon that dimension which we must keep focusing, and above all upon the Lord Jesus Christ himself (i.e. the Giver, not the gifts).

3. The pitfall of manifestation without adoration

There is always a danger of focusing upon the dramatic and spectacular phenomena and losing sight of the Lord Jesus Christ. Again, Frank Bartleman's teaching from the time of the Asuza Street revival can help us here. He wrote in a tract:

> We may not even hold a doctrine, or seek an experience, except in Christ. Many are willing to seek 'power' from every battery they can lay their hands on, in order to perform miracles, draw the attention and adoration of the people to themselves, thus robbing Christ of his glory, and making a fair showing in the flesh. The greatest religious need of our day would seem to be that of true followers of the meek and lowly Jesus. Religious enthusiasm easily goes to seed. The human spirit so predominates, the show-off, religious spirit. But we must stick to our text, Christ. He alone can save. The attention of the people must be first of all, and always, held to him.

Whenever our eyes are taken off the Crucified and Risen Lord Jesus, we will almost certainly be guilty of seeking the spectacular and forgetting the wonderful. More than that, we will be guilty of operating in the flesh. As Bartleman reminds us,

> The Holy Ghost never draws our attention from Christ to himself, but rather reveals Christ in a fuller way.

So a key question we must keep asking is this: 'Are our meetings causing us to be lost in wonder, love and praise concerning the nature and the works of the Lord Jesus?'

Moving Forward

After a recent lecture at an Anglican theological college, two students approached me. One was a Polish Pentecostal. The other was a Pentecostal pastor from India. Both informed me that the ecstatic phenomena associated with the Toronto blessing were unfamiliar to them in their own cultural contexts – even as Pentecostals. They had not seen ecstatic laughter, or drunken behaviour, or wild bodily movements, in churches in the Eastern bloc countries, nor in the rural Indian churches. They had seen it in England, to be sure. They had even experienced it in England. But they were quite convinced that the ecstatic phenomena which we are witnessing today are in fact part of the cultural dimension of the work of the Spirit. They are, as I wrote earlier, the wrapping, not the gift itself – the form, not the actual content.

This needs to be constantly kept in mind as we continue to bless what the Father is doing amongst us. God always operates in a guise which is appropriate to the culture concerned. Since ours is a highly ecstatic culture, I believe that he has graciously adapted his ministry of the Spirit to the needs of the hour. But this does not mean that the manifestations of the Spirit amongst us are to be elevated in terms of importance. They are perhaps the least significant part of the Toronto blessing. Some readers may discern a potential irony here. 'If they're that insignificant, why are you devoting several chapters to them?' The truth of the matter is that my purpose is not to prioritize phenomena except as a way of highlighting that they are the most ephemeral characteristics of a revival. They are the least durable features of a major move of the Holy Spirit. What is really crucial, as we saw in the last chapter, is the fruit of these experiences. It is transformation, not manifestation, that counts.

FOR FURTHER STUDY

Read the following extract from the *Daily Mail*, dated Thursday 4 August 1994. In many ways it is typical of the hundreds of pieces which have appeared in the national press during the year.

1 What is the tone of the reporter?

2 What do you make of the headline?

3 What kinds of phenomena are being reported here?

4 Is this the power of God, as the vicar claims?

5 Is it the kind of place where you would expect these kinds of manifestations?

6 Is there transformation as well as manifestation here?

7 What role do psychological and environmental factors play in such phenomena?

8 What do you make of the last paragraph?

Blessed are the fallen at St James
All was going smoothly at the Sunday prayer meeting.

After the usual songs and readings, the Rev Alistair Kendall invited the congregation of St James to receive the Lord's blessing.

Helen Terry, 36, bowed her head as the 39-year-old vicar passed his hand over her. Then she fell flat on her back, her muscles tensed and eyes flickering wildly. It wasn't the first time. At least 40 of the 100 worshippers at the evangelical church in Bream, Gloucestershire, have collapsed writhing, weeping or giggling during services in the past month.

Others have claimed miraculous cures for long-standing illnesses after being touched by the vicar.

'It's always so sudden and you never know if it is going to happen,' said mother-of-two Mrs Terry, who has since fallen another four times.

Mr Kendall insists that the 'manifestations' have nothing to do with him. 'It's not me – it's the power of God,' he said.

Theology and natural sciences expert Dr Fraser Watts, of Cambridge University, said genuine spiritual processes could be at work.

'But almost always when there is healing there is a psychological element as well,' he said. 'In the centre of a powerful church service, there are highly charged expectations of getting better.'

Spiritual healing can sometimes be a health risk. Officials now stand by at services to catch those overcome as they fall.

chapter four

Extraordinary Phenomena

As we saw in chapter 3, every revival leads to manifestations which are, at first sight, strange. For example, reading
Frank Bartleman's eye-witness narrative called *What Really
Happened at Asuza Street?* (first published in 1925), it is very
quickly clear that some of the phenomena experienced in
worship during the Pentecostal revival were unexpected and
novel. Strangely enough it is not the gift of *glossolalia* or
tongues which most surprised Bartleman and his contem-
poraries. The thing which really amazed them was the singing
in the Spirit which occurred in public meetings. Since there
had been no prior experience of this phenomenon, nor any
Biblical teaching on the matter, the sudden effusions of Spirit-
inspired song were seen as something of a divine *innovatio*
(Aquinas' term, meaning literally 'new thing'). Thus Bartleman writes:

> No one could understand this 'gift of song' but those who had
> it. It was indeed a 'new song' in the Spirit. When I first heard it
> in the meetings a great hunger entered into my soul to receive
> it. I felt it would exactly express my pent up feelings. I had not
> yet 'spoken in tongues'. But the 'new song' captured me. It
> was a gift from God of high order, and appeared among us
> soon after the 'Asuza' work began. No one had preached it.
> The Lord had sovereignly bestowed it . . . It was exercised, as
> the Spirit moved the possessors, either in solo fashion, or by
> the company. It was sometimes without words, other times in
> 'tongues'. The effect was wonderful on the people. It brought
> a heavenly atmosphere, as though the angels themselves
> were present and joining with us.

All revivals are attended by signs that make people wonder, by
unusual phenomena. At Asuza Street it was principally tongues

and singing in the Spirit. At Toronto it has been weeping, roaring, shaking, trembling, falling, drunkenness in the Spirit, and ecstatic laughter. When any new move of the Holy Spirit occurs it is important that we remember to ask four vital questions concerning unusual phenomena:

1 What is the nature of these experiences?

2 Are they Biblical?

3 Have we witnessed them before in church history?

4 What purpose do they serve?

It is my intention in this chapter to answer these four questions in relation to one particular phenomenon which has been witnessed very regularly since the Toronto blessing began – namely, ecstatic laughter.

Outbreaks of Laughter

If singing in the Spirit felt like a new gift at Asuza Street, laughing with joy has felt like a new gift in Toronto. Indeed, one of the more unusual features of the Toronto blessing is the frequent outbreaks of ecstatic laughter in public meetings. The following report, from the *Daily Telegraph* on Saturday 3 December 1994, is an interesting account of a meeting in which ecstatic laughter broke out. Mick Brown (the reporter) began his piece as follows:

> The woman from an Elim Pentecostal Church in St Albans had travelled 3000 miles to see God, and God, in His infinite wisdom, had rewarded her with a joke.
> She had been lying on the floor outside the Gemini suite of the Regal Constellation Hotel in Toronto for an hour, laughing fit to bust. No, not laughing; she was roaring, her arms flapping helplessly at her sides, tears streaming down her face, as if something seriously, profoundly, weirdly, religiously funny was

crackling through her cerebral circuits, sending her spiralling to the outer limits of hilarity.

This laughter was not confined to one person. As Brown's somewhat cynical narrative progresses, others caught it too, including the preacher Randy Clark:

> The drips of laughter had become a torrent. Now Clark started to chuckle himself, as if intoxicated by the mood of the audience. He fought to make himself heard above the rising chorus of guffaws and belly-laughs, cries and groans.

Most remarkable of all, even the reporter himself became affected:

> I found myself beside John Arnott, who was moving through the crowd, blessing people, who fell like ninepins. I didn't even see his hand coming as it arched through the air and touched me gently – hardly at all – on the forehead. 'And bless this one, Lord . . .' I could feel a palpable shock running through me, then I was falling backwards, as if my legs had been kicked away from underneath me. I hit the floor – I swear this is the truth – laughing like a drain.

Laughter in Church

Since the Toronto blessing started, laughter is perhaps the most unusual phenomenon witnessed in meetings. It has been heard and reported all over the place. It is this fact, I suspect, which has accounted for the interest on the part of the media and the public. Church, after all, has not been renowned for 'being a laugh'. Christians as a whole have a reputation for being 'killjoys'. God is not perceived as being fun as well as serious. Worship has not been experienced as playful celebration as well as dutiful reverence. For centuries people with dead-pan faces have been declaring, 'Make thy chosen people joyful', whilst simultaneously repressing the very emotions which might have produced such a holy ebullience. Most would agree with Chuck Swindoll:

> Visit most congregations today and search for signs of happiness and sounds of laughter and you often come away disappointed. Joy, 'the gigantic secret of the Christian', is conspicuous by its absence.

The situation, however, is now changing. There is a good deal of laughter going on in many churches and this feels to many like something new in God's dealings with us. However, it is important for us to realize that this phenomenon is not totally new. There were outbreaks of laughter at Asuza Street when the first wave broke, and countless people were filled with unspeakable love for God. Frank Bartleman says of a number of those converted in the Asuza Street missions that 'During that time they sang, prayed, clapped their hands, rolled about, or sat still.' We ought also to note the fact that ecstatic laughter broke out in 1907 during the revival centred upon Rev. Alexander Boddy. When I visited Pastor Ken Gott at the Sunderland Christian Centre, he told me that he had a computer-enhanced newspaper cutting of an interview with a man who had experienced outrageous joy at one of Boddy's meetings. The headline was, 'The Happiest Day of My Life', and the story was all about the man's experience of hysterical laughter.

Ecstatic laughter therefore broke out during the first wave of the Spirit (Pentecostalism). Indeed, I found the following observation in the entry under 'Slain in the Spirit' in the *Dictionary of Pentecostal and Charismatic Movements*:

> Characteristics of the 'blessing' of being 'slain in the Spirit' include a loss of feeling or control; sometimes those who fall under the power reportedly feel no pain, even if they bump their heads on the way down should 'catchers' fail to do their job. On many occasions the experience is accompanied by

tongue-speech; *at other times laughing*, weeping, or praising of God are manifest (my emphasis).

When we come to the second wave of the Spirit in the twentieth century, the Charismatic renewal in the 1960s, ecstatic laughter is again witnessed. Rev. Philip Smith (see chapter 2) told me recently that he remembers a curate breaking into laughter on receiving what he called 'the baptism in the Holy Spirit'. Philip stresses, however, that this was rare, though one notable incident is recorded for us by Francis MacNutt:

> I particularly remember one conference for Roman Catholic charismatic renewal in England held at Hopwood Hall in the mid-70s. At the end of the conference our team was asked to pray a blessing for the six leaders of their National Service Committee. This is a fairly ordinary request and our team started going down the line of leaders as they stood facing the 350 people in the auditorium. When we got to the second person he fell back unexpectedly as we prayed. Then he burst into loud laughter. The same thing happened with the third, fourth, fifth and sixth leaders. They all lay on the platform roaring with laughter, with the soles of their feet sticking out at the audience. Within minutes most of the 350 conferees were dissolved in gales of laughter.

As we observed in chapter 1, a third wave of the Holy Spirit broke upon the churches in the 1980s. This time the movement of the Spirit was mainly targeted at Protestant Evangelicals, and seemed to have been at least in part to do with the integration of Word and Spirit. During this third wave, unusual manifestations of the Spirit's presence were again visible. Ecstatic laughter was sometimes witnessed. Indeed, I recall one man laughing with infectious enthusiasm at the John Wimber conference in Sheffield in 1985. John Wimber quickly explained that this was the overflow of a heart filled with a new joy in the Lord. Since then I have seen further occasional outbreaks of such holy laughter in meetings like this. Indeed, Francis McNutt (whose books profoundly influenced John Wimber), has written:

> When joy is exuberant enough it bursts out in laughter.
> Laughter is less common than tears at our meetings and
> usually expresses the wonderful relief of finding oneself free of
> a long-standing depression or pain. When someone starts
> laughing – not hysterically, but the deep belly-laugh welling up
> from true happiness – it is really a magnificent experience.
> Usually the spirit of joy is contagious and soon the whole
> room is filled with laughter as, one by one, the entire
> congregation joins in (*Overcome by the Spirit*, p. 79).

Laughter has therefore broken out in the churches before. But what is new now is the frequency and ubiquity of ecstatic laughter. Indeed, even Theological College principals are experiencing it. Rev. Graham Cray's testimony concerning what happened at a New Wine meeting bears this out:

> I found myself swaying, and I don't remember starting. After a
> while I began to laugh from the depths of my gut. The bit of
> me that is analytical was listening and looking, wondering what
> was happening; my emotions were the last part of me to be
> touched. I never felt that my sense of self-control was being
> overridden. I always felt that what was happening had not
> been initiated by myself, and that I could have stopped it had I
> wished, but I could find no reason to stop. There was a deep
> sense of personal liberation.
>
> The immediate aftermath is not that I have laughed more,
> but when I have found myself dealing with situations in a very
> broken world, I have found that tears have been nearer the
> surface. What was a releasing experience of the Holy Spirit
> has, I think, brought me nearer to a feeling of God's heart over
> his world. The laughter has served to make the tears easier.

The Complexity of Laughter
• •

When we are confronted by a strange phenomenon like ecstatic laughter we need to reflect on it both Biblically and theologically. We must be careful not to indulge in a superficial credulity in which anything goes in public acts of worship. We must be careful to test what we see in the light of what we know of both Scripture and the power of God. So what is this laughter in the churches?

In reflecting on this phenomenon we should begin with the recognition that laughter is very difficult to talk about objectively. Karl-Josef Kruschel has recently published a book entitled *Laughter: A Theological Reflection* in which he makes this point forcibly. He writes that 'no scientific theory and no church power has ever really been able to categorize or even control laughter'. Indeed, 'writing a phenomenology of laughter is like dancing on a volcano'. One of the reasons for this is that there are so many different 'spirits' [sic] of laughter. As Kruschel puts it:

> There is joyful, comfortable, playful and contented laughter and there is mocking, malicious, desperate or cynical laughter. There is laughter for sheer pleasure in life and laughter from sheer bitterness at disappointments. There is affirmative, enthusiastic laughter and there is laughing at, ridiculing, on the verge of arrogance and mockery. There is proud laughter and infectious laughter, sick laughter and healing laughter.

In speaking of the ecstatic laughter in churches today it is important to stress the complexity of this phenomenon. As we will see shortly, ecstatic laughter as a charismatic experience may be of different kinds. In discussing this manifestation of the Spirit it is therefore imperative that we remember the words of Jonathan Edwards, who also witnessed ecstatic laughter on occasions during the Great Awakening. Writing of the different ways in which people were moved in their 'affections' during his own day, he stated:

Their joyful surprise has caused their hearts as it were to leap,
so that they have been ready to break forth into laughter,
tears often at the same time issuing like a flood, and
intermingling a loud weeping. Sometimes they have not been
able to forbear crying out with a loud voice, expressing their
great admiration. The manner of God's work on the soul,
sometimes especially, is very mysterious.

'The manner of God's work on the soul . . . is very mysterious.'
We would do well to keep that in mind as we speak of the
complex and unusual phenomenon of *ecstatic laughter*.

What does the Bible say?

If we are to develop some theological foundations for assessing
this experience we must use the Bible as our guide. Contrary to
what has been said by some more sceptical observers, there
are many verses in the Bible concerning laughter. I have discovered the following references using computer word-search
technology:

Genesis 17:17:   Then Abraham fell on his face and
laughed, and said to himself, 'Shall a
child be born to a man who is a hundred
years old? Shall Sarah, who is ninety
years old, bear a child?'

Genesis 18:12:   So Sarah laughed to herself saying,
'After I have grown old, and my
husband is old, shall I have pleasure?'

Genesis 18:13:   The LORD said to Abraham, 'Why did
Sarah laugh and say, "Shall I indeed
bear a child, now that I am old"'?

Genesis 18:15:   But Sarah denied, saying 'I did not

laugh'; for she was afraid. He said, 'No, but you did laugh'.

Genesis 21:6: And Sarah said, 'God has made laughter for me; everyone who hears will laugh over me'.

Genesis 38:23: And Judah replied, 'Let her keep the things as her own, lest we be laughed at'.

2 Chronicles 30:10: So the couriers went from city to city through the country of E'phraim and Manas'seh, and as far as Zeb'ulun; but they laughed them to scorn and mocked them.

Job 5:22: At destruction and famine you shall laugh, and shall not fear the beasts of the earth.

Job 8:21: He will fill your mouth with laughter, and your lips with shouting.

Job 22:19: The righteous see it and are glad; the innocent laugh them to scorn.

Job 39:18: When she rouses herself to flee, she laughs at the horse and his rider.

Job 39:22: He laughs at fear, and is not dismayed; he does not turn back from the sword.

Job 41:29: Clubs are counted as stubble; he laughs at the rattle of javelins.

Psalm 2:4: He who sits in the heavens laughs; the LORD has them in derision.

Psalm 37:13:	But the LORD laughs at the wicked, for he sees that his day is coming.
Psalm 52:6:	The righteous shall see, and fear, and shall laugh at him . . .
Psalm 59:8:	But thou, O LORD, dost laugh at them; thou dost hold the nations in derision.
Psalm 80:6:	Thou dost make us the scorn of our neighbours and our enemies laugh among themselves.
Psalm 126:2:	Then our mouth was filled with laughter, and our tongue with shouts of joy.
Proverbs 1:26:	I also will laugh at your calamity; I will mock them when panic strikes you.
Proverbs 14:13:	Even in laughter the heart is sad, and the end of joy is grief.
Proverbs 29:9:	If a wise man has an argument with a fool, the fool only rages and laughs, and there is no quiet.
Proverbs 31:25:	Strength and dignity are her clothing, and she laughs at the time to come.
Ecclesiastes 2:2:	I said of laughter, 'It is mad'.
Ecclesiastes 3:4:	A time to weep and a time to laugh . . .
Ecclesiastes 7:3:	Sorrow is better than laughter.

Ecclesiastes 7:6: For as the crackling of thorns under a pot, so is the laughter of the fool; this also is vanity.

Ecclesiastes 10:19: Bread is made for laughter, and wine gladdens life, and money answers everything.

Lamentations 1:7: Her enemies looked at her and laughed at her destruction.

Ezekiel 23:32: Thus says the LORD God: 'You shall drink your sister's cup which is deep and large; you shall be laughed at and held in derision, for it contains much.'

Habakkuk 1:10: At kings they scoff, and of rulers they make sport. They laugh at every fortress, for they heap up earth and take it.

Matthew 9:24: He said, 'Depart; for the girl is not dead but sleeping.' And they laughed at him.

Mark 5:40: And they laughed at him.

Luke: 6:21: Blessed are you that weep now, for you shall laugh.

Luke 6:25: Woe to you that laugh now, for you shall mourn and weep.

Luke 8:53: And they laughed at him.

James 4:9: Be wretched and mourn and weep. Let your laughter be turned to mourning and your joy to dejection.

Laughter Prohibited

In our attempt to make sense of all this disparate material, let us begin with the last of these references, James 4:8–10:

> Come near to God and he will come near to you. Wash your hands, you sinners, and purify your hearts, you double-minded. Grieve, mourn and wail. Change your laughter to mourning and your joy to gloom. Humble yourselves before the Lord and he will lift you up.

What is the meaning of these words? In answering this question we must recall the letter as a whole. The letter known simply as 'James' is written as a consequence of division in the church. Christians in the fellowship are indulging in fights, quarrels and slander. What was all this arguing over? The bone of contention seems to have been wealth. The rich were thinking of themselves too highly and despising the poorer brethren (1:9–10). They were actively encouraging a bias to the wealthy (2:1–4) and were neglecting the poor. Indeed, they had forgotten that true religion is about looking after the helpless (1:27) and had neglected the royal law, 'Love your neighbour as yourself' (2:8).

It is into this situation that James says, 'Change your laughter to mourning' (4:9). What kind of laughter is signified here? The laughter James is referring to is the laughter of affluent and apathetic Christians – a mocking laughter directed at the poor, an idle laughter deriving from complacency and indulgence. To people who laugh in this way, James says, 'Change your laughter into the mourning of true repentance'. As he goes on to say,

> Now listen, you rich people, weep and wail because of the misery that is coming upon you. Your wealth has rotted . . .
> (James 5:1–2).

In other words, James is not saying 'There should be no

laughter in church'. Far from it. He is saying that those who laugh with derision because they are affluent, selfish and arrogant must stop laughing and start weeping. Indeed, the command in Greek (*palaiporesate*) is stronger than that; it literally means 'Be miserable!'

James 4:9 is therefore a warning against the mocking laughter of the self-satisfied. No longer are such Christians to rejoice in their apparent superiority. They are to mourn and change their ways. The dangers inherent in ignoring this word of command are severe indeed. In Luke 6:25 the consequences of disobeying such a divine imperative are spelt out by the Lord Jesus himself. Here he utters a prophetic proclamation of disaster upon all those who will not change:

Woe to you who are well fed now,
  for you will go hungry.
Woe to you who laugh now,
  for you will mourn and weep.

Mocking Laughter

With these words of Jesus we can begin to find some precision. The verb translated 'laugh' in this quotation is *gelao*, which is used in two senses from the time of Homer onwards. On the one hand the words *gelao* (I laugh) and *gelos* (laughter) can refer to joyful laughter. On the other hand they can refer to mocking or scornful laughter. The Greek translation of the Old Testament (known as the LXX or the Septuagint) almost always uses *gelao/gelos* in the sense of mocking and superior laughter. If you look at the Old Testament references cited above, you will find this nuance of derision is often visible in the English translations. Yahweh is said to laugh with derision at his enemies. Israel's enemies laugh with derision at the people of God. Sometimes Israel herself laughs her enemies to scorn. In the majority of cases, *gelao/gelos* is used with a derogatory connotation.

When we come to the New Testament the references reveal an interesting development in this theme of scornful laughter. Obviously James says that we are not permitted to laugh in this way if our laughter is motivated by materialistic one-upmanship. Jesus, however, does permit a certain kind of scornful laughter on the lips of Christian men and women. The reference is Luke 6:21 which is expressed in the form of a macarism or beatitude: 'Blessed are you that weep now, for you shall laugh.' Here the verb translated 'laugh' is the Greek word *gelao* which, as we have already noted, most frequently connotes mocking laughter. So what is Jesus saying here? He is basically pointing to that future age when the people of God will be blessed with victory. As the enemies of the church are defeated, the tables will be turned. Having laughed with derision at Christians, Christians will laugh with derision at them! So whilst James prohibits the mocking laughter which stems from materialistic pride, Jesus permits the mocking laughter which stems from the knowledge of ultimate victory.

Joyful Laughter

I wrote earlier that *gelao/gelos* are also used of free and joyous laughter since the time of Homer. Is there a joyful counterpart to mocking laughter in the Bible? The answer to that is yes. We should note the laughter of Sarah in Genesis 21:6:

> God has brought me laughter (*gelota*, LXX), and everyone who hears about this will laugh with me (*sugchareitai*, LXX).

Here the connotation of the word *gelos* is one of joyous and free laughter. The Lord has given happy laughter to Sarah because of her safe delivery of a baby boy in her old age – a boy aptly named 'Isaac', meaning 'He laughs'. Sarah's response is one of ecstatic, spontaneous and heart-felt laughter. She rejoices in the miracle of the gift of Isaac.

It is interesting to note that the LXX translator of the

Hebrew text chose not to use the verb *gelao* when referring to the laughter of Sarah's friends but preferred to use the verb *sugchairo*, which means literally 'to rejoice with someone'. 'Everyone who hears about this will laugh joyfully with me (*sugchareitai*)', says Sarah. Presumably the reason why the translator preferred *sugchairo* to *gelao* is because he knew that the latter had the connotation of derision and he wanted to avoid creating the impression that this laughter was of the cynical sort. Instead he chose a verb with the word *chara* or 'joy' at the heart of it. It is interesting to note that the same word is used by Luke when he describes Elizabeth's neighbours sharing in the joy (*sugchairo*) of the birth of John the Baptist (Luke 1:58). He also uses this verb when describing the shepherd who, when he finds his lost sheep, calls his colleagues to rejoice with him (Luke 15:6) and also when he relates the woman calling her friends together to rejoice with her over the rediscovery of one lost coin (Luke 15:9).

From these observations we can see how there are two kinds of laughter in the Bible. There is the mocking laughter for which the normal Greek words are *gelao/gelos* and the joyous laughter for which the normal Greek word is one involving *chara*, 'joy'. One good example of the latter can be found in Psalm 126, a song of joy celebrating the return to Jerusalem after the Babylonian captivity. The first half of the Psalm is a celebration of the act of homecoming (vv. 1–3). The second is couched in the form of a petition, a prayer that the process of restoration would be completed (vv. 4–6).

When the Lord brought back the captives to Zion,
  we were like men who dreamed.
Our mouths were filled with laughter,
  our tongues with songs of joy.
Then it was said among the nations,
  'The Lord has done great things for them.'
The Lord has done great things for us,
  and we are filled with joy.

Restore our fortunes, O Lord,
   like streams in the Negev.
Those who sow in tears
   will reap with songs of joy.
He who goes out weeping, carrying seed to sow,
   will return with songs of joy, carrying sheaves with him.

In these two beautiful stanzas we catch a glimpse of the kind of laughter which is of the joyful rather than the mocking kind. This is the laughter of homecoming. The people had been in exile and had been in captivity. Now the Lord had set them free, and the people found themselves in a reverie of ecstatic joy: 'we were like men who dreamed'. More than that, not only had the Lord liberated his people, he had brought them home to Israel and the city of Jerusalem. In celebration of their return, their mouths were filled with laughter. To emphasize the fact that this was joyful rather than mocking laughter, the LXX translator of the Hebrew does not write, 'our mouths were filled with *gelos*', but rather, 'our mouths were filled with *chara*'! The Greek translation therefore leaves us in no doubt but the Israelites expressed their untrammelled happiness in joyful laughter. From the overflow of their hearts came giggling, chuckling, guffawing – just about every possible expression on the spectrum of cheerful laughter. In the words of Lewis Carroll, they truly chortled in their joy!

Talking about experience

Talk about 'joy' brings us closer to the point where we can begin to speak meaningfully of the experience of ecstatic laughter. Before we can do that, however, some comments are in order concerning the slippery concept of 'experience' itself.

At the moment there is an interesting debate going on involving an academic theologian called George Lindbeck. In his book, *The Nature of Doctrine: Religion and Theology in a*

Postliberal Age (1984), Lindbeck argues that we cannot use the concept of experience in theology. He believes that religion does not consist of us describing our inner experience of God. Lindbeck argues that we do not have any inner experience of God anyway. What we have is a system of God-talk which is part of our culture, and that defines our experiences. Religion is therefore not the expression of experience. Experience is the expression of religion!

What Lindbeck is driving at is this: we do not have religious experiences which we then express in language and symbol. Rather, our culture provides us with a system of religious language and symbols which then create our experience. So Lindbeck might argue that the experience of tongue-speaking in Asuza Street was not an experience which resulted in a theology (expressed in language), but was rather the product of various people preaching about tongues, which then created the experience. In other words, the experience of tongues was the product of preaching about tongues, not vice versa.

My main problem with Lindbeck's thesis is that it appears sophisticated but is, in reality, simplistic. If we look at people's recent experience of ecstatic laughter as an example, we might justly ask, 'What came first? People talking about laughter or the experience itself?' The honest answer to that question seems to me to be the experience. Some may be guilty of creating an experience on the basis of what they have heard. In reality, however, matters are more complex than this. In many situations, the laughter clearly came first. The experience preceded the talking. This applies to other phenomena as well. We might well refer back to the phenomenon mentioned earlier in this chapter, 'Singing in the Spirit'. That appeared at Asuza Street without anyone preaching about it at all, as Frank Bartleman emphasizes:

> It was a gift from God of the high order, and appeared among us soon after the 'Asuza' work began. No one had preached it. The Lord had sovereignly bestowed it.

The same, we might add, goes for the current prevalence of ecstatic laughter. Indeed, one of the significant things about the present work of the Spirit is that people have not found it easy to put into words the things they are experiencing. As John Arnott and other members of the Vineyard Church have often stated, many of the experiences are very mysterious. Many feel that they have no theological map to guide them.

The Dimensions of Experience

So how can we speak meaningfully about experiences such as ecstatic laughter?

Let us begin by making a distinction between active and passive experiences. An active experience is something which I engineer. It is something which I make happen. So, the experience of heading a football into the back of a net consists of me jumping to meet a cross and directing the ball in a certain direction. I initiate the experience. In many ways, in spite of the variables involved, I direct the experience. The only respect in which I am passive is in relation to the person crossing the ball. I depend on that person to put the ball in the right spot for me to make the complete experience happen.

Whilst some experiences are active, others are passive. They happen to me. The German theologian Jurgen Moltmann describes these passive experiences as 'primary'. He writes:

> Primary experience is something that 'happens to us', something that overpowers us without our intending it, unexpectedly and suddenly. When something like this happens to us, the centre of the determining subject is not in us – in our consciousness or our will; it is to be found in the event that 'befalls' us, and in its source.

When we speak about ecstatic laughter, we are talking about a passive, primary experience. People who have experienced this phenomenon have broken into rapturous laughter suddenly and unexpectedly. It is something which has happened to them, not something which they have made happen. Furthermore, those who have been overwhelmed in this manner regard the source of that experience as outside of themselves – as the work of the Holy Spirit who has invaded their hearts with his life-giving and liberating energy.

This brings me to another point. We need to differentiate between the internal and the external dimensions of experience. An experience can impact me internally, it can change me in the innermost parts of my being. This in turn can affect me externally. The same is true the other way round. Something can happen to me externally (like, for example, being hit by a falling brick) which then affects me internally (anger at the person who dropped it). When it comes to the experience of ecstatic laughter, we must attend to both dimensions, as the following testimony reveals.

Anne Pringle:

Before giving an account of my experience at Sunderland Christian Centre, it is important to give the reader some idea of my previous beliefs or 'Where I'm coming from'.

Since becoming a Christian some three years ago, I have hovered in the background of church activities, being reluctant to commit myself totally to something which may demand more than I was prepared to give. My 'vision' of God was one that was not intrusive or directive. I could be with him on Sundays in church and then put him away for the rest of the week.

I had previously witnessed people, falling over, speaking in tongues, speaking words of knowledge, at a day led by Ann Watson in Newcastle. Whilst interesting to observe, I believed these activities to be based on hysteria and autosuggestion, and consequently dismissed them. I was of the opinion that my view was right, it was safe, my God would not cause me to behave in such a manner.

More recently I heard reports of similar happenings in

Sunderland. Disturbing reports which stated that meetings are held six nights a week, with growing attendance, not the 'one off' that I had attended previously. I was invited to attend Sunderland Christian Centre with some Christian friends who attend the same church as myself. I accepted the invitation with a mixture of curiosity and unease. However I decided that there must be safety in numbers, so nothing terrible could happen to me!

I was amazed at the number of people present, 600 plus. The worship began with songs of praise and with requests for the presence of the Holy Spirit. There was an air of expectation which was almost tangible. At this point there was some evidence of manifestations of the Holy Spirit, but I certainly wasn't too sure about what was happening. There was laughter, repetitive clapping, muscle spasms and crying.

I began to feel very uncomfortable. I felt that the congregation were being whipped to a frenzy by the leaders, and that the 'manifestations' were a consequence of this. It all fitted in quite nicely with my theory, and mentally I took an enormous step back from it all and became an onlooker. I wanted no part of such hysteria, and I certainly did not want to be involved in anything over which I had no control.

Eventually the worship came to an end and it was announced that there would be a time of ministry. More uncomfortable feelings – what now? Everyone seemed to be standing around and there was a team of people praying with individuals. As the ministry progressed, some people fell to the floor, laughing, crying, shaking. The atmosphere had lost its sense of hysteria and expectancy, everything was calm and quiet.

Then, suddenly, a member of the ministry team was praying for me, calling on the Holy Spirit to 'give her what she wants'. In the midst of musing on what it was that I wanted, I realized that I was lying on the floor – flat on my back! How did that happen to me? Someone who has perfect control – confusion! Confusion was rapidly replaced as my whole being was bathed in a dazzling light. Then, very gently, I felt laughter beginning to rise like bubbles to the surface, from deep within me. After some time I began to open my eyes. A friend was praying over me nearby and I clearly remember her saying 'Don't let go, hold on.' I closed my eyes again and the question came back to me 'What is it that I want?'

Everything was suddenly very clear and my answer snapped back 'God, I want God in my life.' I began to shake, gently at first, then uncontrollably. The shaking ceased as suddenly as it had begun, leaving me with the most intense feeling of peace, joy and love that I have ever experienced.

I am aware that there is much criticism of such experiences, and I remain sceptical of some reports. However, I can only tell of my own experience and how it has affected me. I believe that this was a truly spiritual experience, and one that has transformed my faith. The issue isn't about the physical manifestations, it is about what is happening within your own heart.

God is now part of my daily life, we walk hand in hand. It isn't always easy, I don't always want to go where he leads! It would be easier to opt out. But I will not, because he fills my being with love and peace, he is my inspiration, my mentor, my counsellor, my conscience, my friend. With him I know no fear, I am content to do his will.

This story highlights the need to distinguish between active and passive experiences, and between internal and external dimensions. Anne's experience was obviously passive and primary in character. She was not seeking to make anything happen. Indeed, we can discern a good deal of resistance in her narrative. Furthermore, when the experience did occur there was an internal as well as an external dimension to it. As regards her laughing, we ought to note that it began to rise like bubbles to the surface, from deep within her. It was from the inside out, rather than the outside in.

Surprised by Joy
• • • • • • • • • • • • • •

I would like to propose that ecstatic laughter in church is a physical, external response to an experience which is occurring, as it were, on the inside. What is the experience which produces this laughter? It is, in short, one of two things. On the one hand it may be an overwhelming experience of joy. I cannot put it more theologically than that. Ecstatic laughter is in a sense a sacrament. It is an outward and visible sign of an inward and invisible work of grace in my life. As God pours his joy into my heart, my mouth overflows with the two things mentioned in Psalm 126 verse 2: 'laughter and song'. These things – laughter and song – are the external dimensions of an internal, primary experience of unbridled joy.

The phrase which best captures the internal aspect of this experience is 'rejoicing in the Holy Spirit'. Paul makes it clear in Galatians 5:22 that joy is a fruit of the Holy Spirit. Joy is a product of life in the Holy Spirit. As Moltmann has eloquently expressed it:

> When the Spirit of the resurrection is experienced, a person breathes freely, and gets up, and lives with head held high, and walks upright, possessed by the indescribable joy that finds expression in the Easter hymns.

In I Thessalonians 1:6, Paul speaks of 'the joy of the Holy Spirit' (the best attested reading of this verse). This theme of 'rejoicing in the Spirit' is omnipresent in Luke-Acts, as the Pentecostal scholar James Shelton has revealed. Shelton looks at Luke 10:21 and shows how Luke portrays Jesus 'rejoicing in the Spirit' when the 72 return from the mission field. Luke and his community clearly experienced charismatic joy. Shelton goes on to show that rejoicing is in fact one of Luke's favourite themes. Luke uses the verb 'rejoice' (*agalliao*) more than the other Gospel writers. He also uses *chara* (joy), *chairo* (to rejoice) and *synchairo* (to rejoice together) more than the rest, and has an obvious fondness for words related to rejoicing and praise (such as *doxa, doxazo, eucharisteo, aineo, eulogeo, euphraino*). It is this experience of euphoric joy in the Lord which lies at the heart of some of the laughter witnessed in the churches today.

On the other hand, there is another possible internal stimulus for some of the laughter we have witnessed. Looking back over some of the Biblical references to laughter mentioned earlier it is immediately evident that some laughter is joyful (such as Sarah's) whilst other laughter is derisory. As far as the latter is concerned, Jesus himself promises that we will have our tears of oppression transformed into the laughter of victory (Luke 6:21). This laughter will be the superior, scornful laughter of the one who knows for sure that victory and vindication are at hand. Hence Luke's preference in Luke 6:21 for the verb *gelao* rather than *chairo, euphraineo, agaillio*. My own view is that some of the laughter of those which is being heard at the moment is the laughter of hope. It is the laughter of those who are on the front lines of battle, carrying the scars of warfare, yet who are at the same time infused with such a sense of victory that they are overflowing with *gelos*, scornful derision over the enemy in all his insidious manifestations.

Nature and Grace
* * * * * * * * * * * * * * * * *

There are those, however, who argue that these emotions of joy and hope should not be expressed publicly in the form of ecstatic laughter. Such people approve of the internal experience but disapprove of any overt demonstration in public worship. Such a view is probably influenced by one of two factors (or both):

1 The Enlightenment rejection of emotions

The Age of Reason so revered the rational that the emotional was either neglected or repressed. Christians affected by the Enlightenment dichotomy of reason and emotion do not like ecstatic laughter in church. They want a rational, cerebral, doctrinal Christianity in which emotion is kept firmly in its place. They would agree with Hobbes who said, 'Laughing is a bad infirmity of human nature, which every thinking mind would strive to overcome.'

2 The English reserve concerning feelings

Many people in England have learnt to repress strong feelings. This is particularly evident at funerals, where we repress our natural emotions of grief in a most unhealthy way. But laughter is no exception to the rule either. Certainly ecstatic laughter would not be welcome in circles where middle-class respectability is the norm. Many would agree with Lord Chesterfield who said, 'In my mind, there is nothing so illiberal and so ill-bred, as audible laughter.'

Those who say yes to joy and hope but no to ecstatic laughter need to understand that they are operating from a cultural rather than a Biblical point of view. Forbidding genuine, ecstatic laughter in church is just another way of divorcing nature from grace – of divorcing the gracious, undeserved experience of the Spirit in the inner man from its outer, physical manifestations. That is extremely unhealthy. Laughter, as Freud pointed out, is the free discharge of repressed psychical energy. Laughter is therefore a playful liberation, release, and unburdening of powerful emotions in our interior lives. If we deny people the opportunity of expressing emotion in the form of ecstatic laughter we will simply add one more snowfall to the controlling, oppressive winterland of the church. With ecstatic laughter we learn to celebrate our physicality. We learn to play like children. We learn to enjoy our freedom in Christ.

The Nuances of Joy and Hope

Charismatic joy or hope is therefore the internal dimension, ecstatic laughter is the external dimension of the experience I am describing. I want now to look at some of the different nuances of these two inner experiences which stimulate ecstatic, rapturous laughter. The following seem to me to be relevant.

1. The Joy of Homecoming

Teachers at the Airport Vineyard have helpfully suggested that this present movement of the Spirit is more to do with the homecoming of prodigal Christians than with the conversion of unconverted people. Though there are reports of increasing numbers of conversions, this observation does seem to me to be fair. In Luke's account of the prodigal son, the result of his homecoming is celebration. Here Luke uses one of his favourite words, *euphraino*, to describe the party which follows the boy's return. Luke 15:23, 24: 'Let's have a feast and make merry (*euphranthomen*), for this son of mine was dead and is alive again; he was lost and is found.' So they began to make merry (*euphrainesthai*).

This note of celebration is an important clue to our understanding of ecstatic laughter. When the people of Israel came home to Zion their mouths were filled with laughter (Psalm 126:2). When a sinner repents the whole of heaven experiences joy (*chara*, Luke 15:7). It is inconceivable to imagine the father's party in the story of the prodigal son as a party without laughter. Likewise, it is hard to imagine the joy of heaven not involving laughter when one sinner repents, or when one lost sheep is found (Luke 15:6). Sir Thomas Browne spoke of 'that unextinguishable laughter in heaven'. It is precisely that heavenly laughter which is being experienced in people's hearts today as they return in large numbers to a passion for the Kingdom – in short, to their first love for the Lord.

2. The Hope of Victory

In the Kingdom of God there are seasons of costly sowing and seasons of glorious reaping. For many leaders, the recent past has been more a matter of sacrificial sowing. It is my belief that the laughter being witnessed in many churches today stems from a new hope that a time of fruitfulness and victory is at hand. Indeed, there is a very powerful and (I believe) timely prophecy in Psalm 126 verse 6:

> He who goes out weeping, carrying seed to sow,
> will return with songs of joy, carrying sheaves with him.

In my own recent experience I have observed an interesting dynamic in the phenomena associated with the Toronto blessing. When the Spirit comes in power upon a group of people I have frequently witnessed a number of them entering into a period of weeping followed by a time of ecstatic laughter. This kind of laughter obviously has a good deal to do with hope. Where there has been the sorrow of Calvary, God is supplementing it with the laughter of Easter. This is the laughter of victory over the enemy. As Jesus promised,

> Blessed are you who weep now, for you will laugh
> (Luke 6:21).

Laughter and Eschatology

As far as the more derisory kind of laughter is concerned, it is extremely important to understand the dimension of eschatology. Eschatology is a complicated theological term meaning 'the study of the last things'. The word *eschaton* means 'last thing' and *logos* means 'rational discourse'. When we speak about eschatology we are basically focusing on the four last things traditionally associated in Christian theology with the end of the world: the return of Jesus Christ, the last judgement, heaven, and hell.

When Jesus promises in Luke 6:21 that our weeping will be turned to laughing (*gelao*), he does so in the context of the future when his Kingdom will be fully come on earth. Jesus, as we will recall, inaugurated the Kingdom of God in his own ministry. The Kingdom of God is essentially the dynamic rule of God which pushes back the powers of darkness – powers such as poverty, sin, oppression, injustice, sickness and death. In Jesus' own time, this powerful advance of the Kingdom was made manifest in healing, nature and resurrection miracles, as well as in exorcisms and authoritative teaching. Wherever these things happened – either through Jesus himself or through his disciples – the Reign of God was established. However, Jesus also taught that this Divine Kingdom would not be fully consummated in his own lifetime. Rather, it would only be at his return in great glory on the clouds that the Kingdom would be finally and completely established on earth. Until then, the battle between light and darkness would continue unabated, even though ultimate victory is assured for Christians.

When Jesus says that those who weep now will one day laugh, he is doing far more than just quoting a common theme in the Wisdom literature of his day. He is promising us that there will come a day when our enemies will finally be vanquished. That, says Jesus, is a day on which we will 'rejoice' and 'leap for joy' (Luke 6:23). Rejoicing implies some kind of physical expression – singing, shouting, laughing or weeping. Leaping for joy is even more physical. The verb here is *skirtao*, used elsewhere of sheep happily skipping about! The disciples, when the weeping starts to turn to laughter, will be springing about like happy sheep on the hills. As the world's last night draws near, the disciples of Jesus will find the scornful laughter of victory and superiority beginning to flow from their mouths. They will discover the evil one starting to decrease in importance. Jesus alone, and his impending return, will become the exclusive obsession.

A Celebration of Laughter

I hope from these comments that it will now become clear that we are dealing with an extremely complex phenomenon when we talk about 'ecstatic laughter'. Initially I was very sceptical about this unusual behaviour. Indeed, whilst on holiday last August, I happened to watch a cartoon on TV with my three children. The cartoon was *Batman*, and the plot centred on the Joker's attempt to stupefy the whole of Gotham City with a kind of laughter gas. As the cartoon progressed, a chilling thought entered my head. 'What if all the laughter in many churches today is the work of the Arch-Joker, the father of lies? What if the great Trickster himself has found a way of distracting and even crippling hundreds of churches with a kind of supernatural laughter gas?'

This sense of scepticism was not helped by some comments made publicly by Clifford Hill. He wrote of the Toronto blessing:

> The new feature of this phenomenon is laughter. It is often described as joy but most of the reports also indicate that the laughter is often hysterical and even maniacal. Such manifestations are unlikely to be of the Holy Spirit and are more likely to be of the flesh or of an alien spirit.

Hill went on to add,

> Indeed, throughout the Bible, the great majority of references to laughter are associated with scorn, derision or evil.

When I read those words, I was troubled. Within a few weeks, however, I had experienced this ecstatic laughter myself and within several more weeks I was witnessing it in others when I prayed for them. On no occasion have I felt that this laughter was hysterical in the technical, medical sense, let alone 'maniacal'. There have been moments when I questioned some outbursts. Ecstatic laughter, however, is an unusual, complex phenomenon. Some of it is the laughter of victory, in which Christians (particularly church leaders) have rediscovered a blessed assurance of the greatness of Jesus and the smallness of the evil one. This kind of laughter is the derisory *gelos* which scorns and derides the enemy. Other occurrences of this phenomenon seem more like the laughter of joy, in which Christians rediscover their first love and the concomitant joy of their salvation. This kind of laughter is the playful *chara* which celebrates a newfound, childlike intimacy with the Father, the Son and the Holy Spirit.

Laughter is therefore a manifestation of the Spirit. It is a passive experience. It is something which happens to a person. It is not something which I make happen. It has an internal dimension, insofar as it is the invasion of joy or hope into my spirit which leads to the effusion of ecstatic laughter from my body. It is certainly a Biblical phenomenon. As we saw earlier, there are many Bible passages referring to the mocking laughter of superiority and the joyful laughter of knowing God. There are precedents in church history. Jonathan Edwards witnessed ecstatic laughter. So did Wesley and Whitefield (though they all responded to it differently). There has also been increasing evidence of this unusual phenomenon in our own century. The experience itself, finally, obviously has a point and a purpose. Those who have experienced it have testified that it has been a profound release of tension, a natural expression of joy, and an ebullient liberation of hope. It has, in short, changed them. Given all these facts, we would be unwise to suppress this new springtime of laughter in the church. We must beware of sounding like the strict rabbi who said,

When you have an impulse towards frivolity, then resist it with the words of Torah (c. 300 AD).

The Froth on the Wave

Having said that, it is vital not to overstress the importance of ecstatic laughter. Laughter is a vital way of releasing deep emotions. Indeed, laughter may well be extremely helpful in terms of healing. Many readers may have heard of Norman Cousins' extraordinary story narrated in *Anatomy of an Illness as Perceived by the Patient*. In this book Cousins describes his reaction to the news that he had an incurable illness. He decided on a lifestyle of vitamins, healthy food and laughter therapy. The last of these is interesting. It involved watching funny films, episodes from TV comedy shows and cartoons – basically, everything that he found amusing and which made him laugh. In fact, he discovered that anything which made him laugh for a consistent period of time (about ten minutes) actually relieved the pain from his illness for up to two hours. To the astonishment of the medics, Cousins began to recover and lived many years longer than he was expected to. Truly, a cheerful heart proved to be good medicine (Proverbs 17:22).

Even though ecstatic laughter is liberating and helpful for many who experience it, it is still just a *pneumo-somatic* phenomenon (to use Bishop Michael Marshall's helpful phrase). It is just one outward, physical manifestation of the presence of the *pneuma* or Spirit of God at work in the believer's life. When Henri Bergson wrote the classic work on laughter in 1921 he stressed an important point. Laughter is like the foam on top of a wave. The one who tries to reason about laughter is like a child who draws off the foam with his hands only to find that just a few drops of water pass through his fingers. Bergson was trying to highlight the mysterious nature of laughter in this analogy. But there is another application too. The truth of the matter is that the foam is not the most important part of the wave. The wave itself is, along with its effects. This fact should act as a constant reminder in these exciting days that the most important thing about the fourth wave of the Spirit is not the froth on the top (laughing, roaring, shaking, falling over, weeping and the like) but the wave itself and what it does to both the Church and the world.

The Pitfalls of Ecstatic Laughter

At the end of the last chapter I concluded by mentioning some of the possible pitfalls during times when ecstatic phenomena are prevalent. Laughter is no exception to this. Laughter is a potentially addictive experience. Like eating, it releases natural pain-killers (endorphins) in the structure of the brain, creating a temporary anaesthesia and even euphoria. As such, this experience can, if we are not very careful, become an end in itself. It can become just one more mood-altering, addictive behaviour to add to the vast number already on offer in both the world and the Church. Whilst the Lord does want his children to laugh and rejoice, we must all of us recognize that perpetual happiness is to be enjoyed in heaven not on earth. It is something for the not yet, not for the now of the Kingdom. Indeed, tears rather than laughter are the more usual response in times of revival. A revived church becomes painfully aware of its sinfulness, and of the poignant needs of a fallen world. That usually leads to weeping rather than to laughing.

I believe that it is this deep appreciation of the need for holiness – and indeed of the suffering of the world – which explains John Wesley's acute ambivalence towards ecstatic laughter during his own meetings. In his diary he wrote the following in 1740:

> Friday May 9: I was a little surprised at some, who were buffeted of Satan in an unusual manner, by such a spirit of laughter as they could in no wise resist though it was pain and grief to them. I could scarce have believed the account they gave me had I not known the same thing ten or eleven years ago.

Here the reader can discern a note of uncertainty in Wesley's writing. He regards laughter as an unusual phenomenon ('an unusual manner'). He seems to imply that it is the result of demonic oppression (a 'buffeting by Satan'). Yet he himself had experienced it. Indeed, he was to see it again and not long after:

> Wednesday May 21: In the evening such a spirit of laughter was among us that many were much offended. But all the attention was fixed on poor L. S. whom we all knew to be no dissembler. One so violently and variously torn of the evil one did I never see before.

Wesley was clearly both surprised and alarmed by the outbreaks of what he called 'a spirit of laughter'. When this occurred, he recognized that the person who experienced it was not putting it on. He also recognized that it was an ecstatic experience – that the person had no real control over it. However, he assumed that it was demonic rather than holy in nature. Why did he jump so quickly to this conclusion? I believe there are two purely cultural reasons for this. The first has to do with respectability, a word which became increasingly popular as the eighteenth century wore on. Loud laughter was regarded as socially undignified amongst English gentlemen in this period. Children were taught from a very early age to be seen and not heard. Indeed, Wesley once said, 'He who plays when he is a child, will play when he is a man.' This was to be strenuously resisted, because levity in adults was reprehensible. 'Avoid all lightness as you would avoid hell-fire,' he said. No wonder, then, that 'many were much offended' when ecstatic laughter broke out in the meeting above. No wonder Wesley himself was offended. Wesley had bought into the values of respectability. Childlike play and joyful laughter were not to be part of the normal Christian life, as far as he was concerned.

Secondly, it may be that Wesley took this dismissive attitude towards laughter because one of the chief concerns he had about English society in his own day concerned frivolity. Instead of dealing with the vices of society, many in Wesley's time regarded it as a social duty to reject a 'doom-and-gloom' philosophy, and adopt instead a sense of abandonment, joviality and fun. Thus, even death became a subject of comedy. Indeed, it was during this time that gravestones started to be inscribed with humorous epitaphs – such as this one for Samuel Foote, a one-legged comedian memorialized in Westminster Abbey:

> Here lies one Foote, whose death may thousands save,
> For death has now one foot within the grave.

It is quite probable that Wesley regarded ecstatic laughter as 'demonic' simply because he expected socially respectable behaviour in church, and because he detested the escapist frivolity of men like Erasmus Darwin, the physician, who said: 'In order to feel cheerful you must appear to be so.' There are therefore purely cultural reasons – I would argue – why Wesley was ambivalent about laughter.

In the final analysis I would therefore encourage all of us not to dismiss ecstatic laughter for cultural reasons. We must allow God to be God, and to do in us that which is pleasing to him. Of course we need to guard against counterfeit, demonic laughter, and also against human, exhibitionist laughter. But we must at the same time be careful not to quench the Spirit. Ecstatic laughter was witnessed during previous great movements of the Holy Spirit, as we have seen in this chapter. It is also a phenomenon about which the Scriptures are certainly not silent. We should therefore be careful not to be too controlling in our leadership of meetings where this holy joy and this impassioned hope are expressed so emotionally and so enthusiastically.

FOR FURTHER STUDY

Examine the following testimony from a friend of mine called Tim Fordham. Tim works at the YMCA in Sheffield and has recently been to Toronto.

After reading his story, ask yourself these questions.

1 Which kind of laughter did Tim experience? Was it mocking laughter (*gelos*) or joyful laughter (*chara*)?

2 How easy is it, in practice, to distinguish clearly between these two kinds of laughter?

3 Was this laughter a passive or an active experience?

4 How easy is it, in practice, to distinguish clearly between passive and active experiences?

5 What is the significance of the weeping prior to the laughing?

6 What were the fruits of this experience?

7 Do you regard Tim's experience as Biblical and Spirit-inspired?

Tim Fordham

A few months before we left for Toronto, God had made me many promises during times of prayer. The most significant was a word someone had, that God was going to 'give me the desires of my heart' (Psalm 37:4). I felt this was in relation, for the most part, to my work. I am a hostel manager at Sheffield YMCA, working with young people who have experienced homelessness. Many have been rejected by people, most often parents, who should have provided security and love. Being homeless is a symptom of the abuse they have suffered. I sensed God wanted me and the rest of the team to be motivated by the love of Christ and to understand the potential of God's Holy Spirit to heal broken lives.

There was, however a pre-condition for God to fulfil his promise, which came in the next verse of the Psalm – 'commit your way to the Lord, trust in him and he will act'. As you can imagine I was very excited about all of this and could see the potential for God working in a wonderful and powerful way.

Then the problems started – things became very difficult at work, to the extent that I found it hard to see God working at all – my faith ebbed away. I felt a little like I imagine Joseph to have felt when he was thrown into prison after God had promised him so much.

I didn't realize it at the time, but the reason for coming up against a brick wall was because I had tried to fulfil God's promises for him in my strength, my timing, generally trying too hard and not allowing God room to work. This also meant that I got into old patterns of thinking – doubts crept in and my confidence in God plummeted.

It was at this time that we had the opportunity to travel to Toronto. For the first couple of nights at the Airport Vineyard,

I was still fighting against God, but before the last night I felt God say 'Don't miss out on the blessing I have for you.' 'How do I do that?' I asked. 'Don't do anything, just be open to what I want to give you,' was God's response to my questioning.

The first person who prayed for me that evening enabled God to highlight old hurts that had built up in me, which had become a blockage to God's Holy Spirit. They prayed that God would take away the negative effect of words spoken to me when I was younger, particularly within my family. I believe that these feelings had come back, even though I have received prayer about them, because I had begun to doubt God. They were stronger too because we were visiting my sister in Toronto and we had spoken at some length about our family. I had told none of this to the person praying for me! It was as though God was removing the things which were preventing me from receiving his love.

I waited where I was, because I felt God wasn't finished with me yet! As the next person prayed that I would know God's love for me, I had a strong impression of kneeling before Jesus on the Cross. He was weeping and his tears flowed over my body. I believe, in talking this through afterwards, that God was giving me a gift of intercession by revealing his heart to me.

Now what I needed was the Holy Spirit, to move forward in God's strength instead of my own. As a third person quietly prayed for me, God poured his Spirit on me, releasing tears of joy. He then showed me, as if in a movie, all the situations I had become stressed about and all that overpowered my faith. As he did, God filled me with joy and I was able to laugh long and hard at all of them. This must have gone on for half an hour. God kept revealing something else and I would suddenly burst out laughing. It was as it says in 1 Peter 5:7, I was able to 'cast all my anxiety on him, because he cares for me'. The anxieties seemed so insignificant in the light of God's power and his promises to overcome.

Since that night, I have had doubts and have lacked faith, but God keeps reminding me of what he has done. The fruits of allowing him to work in my life, instead of me trying to call the shots all the time, are beginning to be evident at work, as I have been able to share the Gospel more freely with residents. I find I keep wanting to declare that Jesus is Lord.

chapter five

Essential Preparation

• •

In July of 1994 I was desperate. My own spirituality was one of performance rather than reality. I was leading my church as if I was on fire for the Lord when in truth I was little more than a smouldering wick. More than that, I was standing up at conferences and speaking with a dynamism which owed far more to my flesh than to God's Spirit. I had become a prey to vanity and ambition, and as a consequence was tired, anxious, and depressed. Ministry had become a burden to me. The church where I serve full time was proving to be extremely stressful. Sleep had become a premium. All I could see was the cost of leadership. I had truly become weary in well-doing.

Then, one Thursday afternoon, I decided to phone Bishop David Pytches. One of the many pressure points in my leadership at the time was a particular person who on the surface exercised a very powerful charismatic ministry. Behind the scenes, however, I was beginning to see evidence of manipulation and unaccountability. I phoned David, and he gave me sound advice about dealing with the situation decisively – advice which, in the course of time, has saved a good deal of heartache and upset in the Body of Christ.

At the end of my phone call, David mentioned a small church in Toronto called the Airport Vineyard. Now I knew about Vineyard churches because I had been deeply changed as a result of attending a conference organized by John Wimber (the leader of the Vineyard movement) in Sheffield in 1985. In that conference I had experienced the power of the Holy Spirit for the very first time. I had been a Christian for nearly ten years, but I had never experienced the reality of God like this before. I had grown up amongst conservative evangelicals who regarded supernatural power (particularly the more dramatic spiritual gifts, such as tongues and healing) as at best something for missionaries in poor countries, and at worst, something which died out with the apostles. Here, however, I witnessed the works which, in the New Testament, attended the words. As a result, my understanding, experience and ministry were never to be the same again.

In the years after 1985, things were not easy. My first curacy was in a church with conservative evangelical leadership. The frustration of not being able to apply the lessons and experiences gained at the Signs and Wonders conference was at times unbearable. After four years I was running on empty. God had other plans, however. He moved us on to St Thomas' Crookes in Sheffield, a huge charismatic church attended by well over 1000 people (comprising Anglicans and Baptists) and led by Canon Robert Warren. There my wife Alie and I slowly began a journey of healing and renewal which was to set us on our feet again.

In the summer of 1992 the Lord gave me a word about 'breaking out of comfort zones' and 'living on the edge for Jesus'. I started preaching this message, even though I was not actually living it in any real terms at the time. A few weeks later, however, Alie and I went on holiday with the children. At the time we were both convinced that we were meant to stay at St Thomas' for a very long time. At some point on that holiday, God changed all that. Quite independently of each other Alie and I heard God's call to move on from St Thomas'. I shared that with Alie, and she immediately shared the same burden with me. On our return from holiday, I went to my Bishop and informed him.

Within six months I had become the vicar of St Mark's Grenoside (in Sheffield), a parish which is 'on the edge' both geographically and spiritually. There the constant pressure of doing two jobs (the previous incumbent had a curate; I was on my own), on top of my university lecturing at the Department of Biblical Studies at Sheffield University, quickly exhausted me. There was the added problem of the controlling prophetess mentioned earlier, as well as other evidences of intrigue in the fellowship. By the summer of 1994 I was very dry spiritually, worn out physically, and pretty low emotionally. Everything I

was at that time can be summed up in the melancholy words of
Psalm 63:

> O God, you are my God,
>   earnestly I seek you;
> My soul thirsts for you,
>   my body longs for you,
> In a dry and weary land
>   where there is no water.

It was at this point that David Pytches asked, 'Have you heard
what's been going on at the Airport Vineyard in Toronto?' In
fact I had not. David then proceeded with typical and infectious
enthusiasm to record the events earlier in the year at Toronto –
events which are recorded and published in at least three books,
so there is no need to repeat them here. As he spoke, something
inside told me, 'This is for you.' I was thirsty, I was hungry. I felt
very much as if I was in a desert but that David was pointing me
towards a burning bush.

And so, the following week, I travelled with some friends
down to Holy Trinity Brompton where David was going to be
speaking to a number of church leaders. After a time of songs,
teaching and testimonies, a ministry time began. As I stood
with my hands held out, I felt nothing at all. The problem was
threefold:

1. I had become too used to giving ministry, and, in the
   process, had lost the art of receiving it;
2. I felt distracted by the extraordinary phenomena around me
   (particularly the loud and long outbursts of ecstatic
   laughter);
3. I was seeking to analyse everything, instead of setting my
   mind on what the Spirit desires.

In fact, 45 minutes elapsed before I had worked through each
of these barriers to blessing.

Once I had done that, I found I was much more receptive.
Several members of the ministry team came and prayed for me
and as they did so, my body started to react to the presence of

the Holy Spirit. I started swaying backwards and forwards on my feet. My right arm started shaking. Before long I was on the floor – not because I had been forced there by human hands or even by the Holy Spirit – but simply because that was the safest and most sensible place to be! As I lay there I felt a greater sense of peace, relaxation and quietude than I had for a very long time indeed. I felt the stress and strain physically lift from my body. I closed my eyes and rested in the presence of the Lord.

A few moments later, a woman stepped over me, and on her way towards someone else prayed over me. Within a few moments I felt this great joy at the core of my being. I started to experience a deep sense of 'All shall be well and all manner of thing shall be well' – of blessed assurance that God had all my ministerial problems well under control, and that they were of piffling and minuscule importance in the light of his awesome glory. As this increased I was aware of chuckles starting to well up inside. Before long I was laughing like a child, in absolute hysterics in fact, as the burdens were lifted and as the Spirit refreshed me. Out of the overflow of a joyful heart came holy laughter.

That, for me, was a turning point. On my return to St Mark's, and over the last six months, I have managed to handle some extremely difficult situations with a confidence and a peace that I certainly did not have before. I am much more excited about the future, more joyful about serving the Lord, more in love with Jesus Christ. I have seen the Spirit at work far more powerfully than at any time previously. People who have been oppressed spiritually have received deliverance. Others who have been walking in fear and trepidation as Christians have received a new boldness and authority. Many have been touched by the Spirit and changed as a result. Most exciting of all, new people have started coming to the church.

The Importance of the Desert

The reason I tell that story is not to draw attention to myself but to a point about the importance of the desert in times of revival. It seems to me that the desert experience – that season of weariness, dryness and weakness which all true followers of Christ enter from time to time – is an essential preparation for personal renewal in these days. The truth of the matter is that many of those who are experiencing refreshing from the Lord are doing so after a journey through tiredness, repentance and hunger. There are many stories being told of pastors and leaders who have reached rock bottom, who have recognized that they have been guilty of independence rather than dependence on the Lord, and who have felt lost in the blazing sun of a dry and weary land. For myself I have to say that I had no understanding or experience of the desert before last summer. I had not recognized that for Spirit-filled Christians, times of refining are as important as times of refreshing, that times in the desert feeling fruitless are as important as times in the Jordan getting soaked in the glory! Now, however, one of the things I feel most strongly about is the centrality of the desert experience as we head for revival.

The desert, in fact, is one of the keys to revival. More than that, an understanding of the place of the desert experience in charismatic spirituality is crucial at the present time. The reason I say that is because my own experience, and the experience of many others, is this: that we have been refreshed by the Holy Spirit at the point where we have, in the words of Alcoholics Anonymous, 'hit bottom' and had 'an awakening'. It was at the moment when our own resources ran out, when exhaustion and demoralization set in, that we suddenly had our eyes spiritually opened and we saw our deep and desperate need for a totally God-centred life. For so many of us, particularly pastors and leaders, it has been when we entered a trough of weariness and desperation that the Lord said, 'Come to the waters and drink.' The desert has therefore been an essential preparation for many of us. It has been the place of repentance where we have had to forsake our controlling ways and let the Spirit truly take control.

The desert experience is therefore part of the normal charismatic life. It is part of the Father's plan for all of us. So often

Spirit-filled Christians talk as if the desert experience is a temporary and very rare dip in the graph of a triumphant spirituality. If the desert experience is mentioned by charismatics at all – and it is rarely mentioned – then it is talked about as a kind of taboo subject, as an embarrassing and regrettable interlude. Desert spirituality, we say, is something for fashionable contemplatives. It is not for those of us who live as overcomers. But that is simply a false and un-Biblical assumption. It is a lie which fosters toxic guilt in Spirit-filled Christians who know that times of testing are important for developing maturity in Christ. It is a teaching which is unhelpful to those who may be experiencing a time of discipline from the Father.

The Testing in the Wilderness

Time and again I have found myself drawn back to the same Scripture when thinking about revival. That Scripture is the story of Jesus' experience in the desert, as recorded in Matthew 4:1–11:

> Then Jesus was led by the Spirit into the desert to be tempted by the devil. After fasting for forty days and forty nights, he was hungry. The tempter came to him and said, 'If you are the Son of God, tell these stones to become bread.'
>
> Jesus answered, 'It is written: "Man does not live on bread alone, but on every word that comes from the mouth of God."'
>
> Then the devil took him to the holy city and had him stand on the highest point of the temple. 'If you are the Son of God,' he said, 'throw yourself down. For it is written: "He will command his angels concerning you, and they will lift you up in their hands, so that you will not strike your foot against a stone."'
>
> Jesus answered him, 'It is also written: "Do not put the Lord your God to the test."'
>
> Again, the devil took him to a very high mountain and

showed him all the kingdoms of the world and their
splendour. 'All this I will give to you,' he said, 'if you will bow
down and worship me.'

Jesus said to him, 'Away from me, Satan! For it is written:
"Worship the Lord your God, and serve him only." '

Then the devil left him, and angels came and attended him.

The first important thing to notice about this story is – as
always – the context. Matthew 4:1–11 (the testing of Jesus in
the desert) occurs directly after Matthew 3:13–17 (the baptism
of Jesus at the River Jordan). The story of Jesus' battle with
Satan comes directly after his baptism in water and the Holy
Spirit. Now this fact alone contains a great and profound truth:
that the blessing cannot be divorced from the battle; that being
filled with the Holy Spirit does not mean a life of comfort and
entertainment. It means that there will be times of testing in
the desert as well as times of blessing in the Jordan. Seasons in
the desert are therefore part of our life in the Spirit. Matthew
stresses that when he writes in verse 1, 'Jesus was led by the
Spirit into the desert to be tempted by the devil.' Notice, he
was 'led by the Spirit'. In Mark's version of the same story, the
point is made even more strongly. In Mark's account, Jesus is
'driven out' into the desert by the Holy Spirit (Mark 1:12).
There the Greek word is *ekballo* from which we get the word
'ballistic' (as in 'ballistic missile'). It was therefore the Holy
Spirit who led Jesus there, not Satan. To be sure, it is Satan
who did the testing once Jesus was in the desert. It is
Satan who shows Jesus the stones which look like bread. It is
Satan who takes Jesus to the highest pinnacle of the temple. It
is Satan who takes Jesus to the top of a very high mountain.
But it is the Holy Spirit who leads Jesus into the desert and it is
the Holy Spirit who leads him out. That means the desert experience was God's will for his Son. The same is true for us too.

Secondly, our desert experiences are only supposed to be for
a season. They are not supposed to last the whole of our
Christian lives. If we are obedient to what the Father wants to
do with us in the desert, then we will be able to leave the

wilderness at God's appointed time. For Jesus, the appointed time was 'forty days and forty nights'. Now the number 'forty' may have been partly dictated by the fact that the people of Israel wandered for forty years in their desert experience. It was however wholly dictated by the Father's sovereign plan and purpose. The Father decreed that Jesus' desert trek was to be for just under two months, and no more. He decreed that because there were significant issues which needed addressing during that time – three issues connected with the three temptations. God the Father was allowing his Son to be tested in three areas where our human flesh is particularly prone to disobedience and sin. We will look at those three areas in a moment. The vital thing to see at this juncture is that the Son of God resisted the three temptations courageously and, as a result, was led out of the desert and attended by angels.

The two truths I am therefore stressing are these: that our desert experiences are part of the normal charismatic life, and that they are only for a season. As so often with Scripture, this is a liberating message. Jesus' truths are liberating (John 8:34) and it is always a joyful experience watching people set free by the truth of his Word. This came home to me with particular force when I was recently invited to speak at a church weekend away. The church in question is well-known for its emphasis upon signs and wonders and the power of the Holy Spirit. On the Saturday morning I felt the Lord encouraging me to speak on the story of Jesus' desert trek in Matthew 4:1–11. When I had finished stressing the two truths above, I asked all those who felt as if they were in the desert to stand. About 35 stood up (out of 150). I then told the folk around them to pray, saying 'Father, I bless what you're doing in this person's desert experience' – not, 'Father, bring them out of the desert!' So they prayed as they were told and the effects were quiet but deep. After the weekend I had a number of letters in which people who received prayer spoke about the lifting of guilt from their lives, a greater clarity about what God wanted to do in them, and an increased sense of hope about the future. The desert, they now understood, is part of the normal charismatic life.

But What is the Desert?
* *

The desert is, however, a metaphor. It is not for us a literal, geographical area of arid barrenness as it was for many of the early church contemplatives. Saint Antony (born 251 AD) went into a literal desert, choosing in 285 AD to cross the Nile and enter the wilderness. There he found the ruins of a fortified castle which had a spring of water nearby and passed his time in prayer and in making mats. There he lived with God and fought with demons – a holy man engaging in spiritual warfare in an actual desert. For twenty years he lived like this, stripped of all material clutter, living with the very basic necessities of life and nothing more. His example attracted many, who came to live near him in the baking heat of the desert sun. After a period of intense persecution (in which Antony came out of his place of solitude), this great saint went back into the desert to a remote place near the Red Sea. That place became the monastery of St Antony, which is still in existence today. Antony himself died in 356 AD, at the ripe old age of 105! By the end of the fourth century, there were thousands of monks living in desert communities, living simple lives and doing battle with the principalities and powers – just as Antony had done.

Saint Antony, and many monks after him, entered a literal desert in order to follow the example of Jesus in Matthew 4:1–11. For us today, however, the desert is a metaphor for a particular kind of experience. The experience itself is about repentance and healing. It is a season of our lives in which we become acutely conscious of the barren and fruitless things in the world, the church and in ourselves. We become conscious of sterility as opposed to vitality, of stagnation as opposed to dynamism, of emptiness as opposed to fullness, of compromise as opposed to holiness. We become unable to cover up our weaknesses any longer. Tears flow uninvited from our eyes. Vulnerability becomes the keynote of our lives.

The desert is a season in which we are forced to see things as they really are. This desert can be any number of things. It can be a season of physical illness or depression. It can be a season of stress and anxiety. It can be a season of poverty. It can be a season of spiritual isolation. It can be a season of theological questioning and change. It is always a season of deep refining through repentance. Whatever the actual circumstances, our desert experiences are times when the normal supports of life are removed. We are alone with ourselves, vulnerable and fearful. We see our sins, our hurts, our weaknesses, our failures, our pride, our vanity, our woundedness. In fact, we are confronted at every turn by our shadow. In the desert, there is nowhere we can go to hide from our shadow, and our shadow is the part of us where our sins, hurts and demons have found a home. In the desert we cannot flee from the fiery heat of God's holiness.

In this season of clarity, we face the facts and make ourselves vulnerable to the Great Physician. As we come to that awakening, we can choose to let the Lord heal us of our wounds, to cleanse us from our sins, and to deliver us from the darkness which has come to cling to us so relentlessly. We can learn to let go of our sinful ways in tearful repentance. We can relinquish our desire to control both the Lord and ourselves, and hand over our lives to the control of the one with the highest power, Jesus Christ. As we do that, the drought comes to an end. The Father, in his own way and at his own timing, graciously leads us out of spiritual, emotional and physical weariness into a personal renewal in which our first love is rekindled. In the process, the promises of Isaiah 35 become gloriously fulfilled in our spiritual experience:

> The desert and the parched land will be glad;
> The wilderness will rejoice and blossom.
> Like the crocus, it will burst into bloom;
> It will rejoice greatly and shout for joy.

The First Temptation

What are the things which the Lord deals with in the desert of refining? Here we need to return to the story of Jesus' wilderness experience in Matthew 4:1–11. Jesus is subjected to three tests in the desert, all of them highly relevant to our situation today. The first temptation can be summed up in the phrase: *charismatic egoism*, by which I mean, the use of spiritual power for oneself rather than for others. Matthew narrates this temptation as follows:

> After fasting for forty days and forty nights, Jesus was hungry. The tempter came to him and said, 'If you are the Son of God, tell these stones to become bread.'
>
> Jesus answered, 'It is written: Man does not live on bread alone, but on every word that comes from the mouth of God.'

It is important at this point to stress that the temptations of Jesus are not directed at his sonship. The NIV translation, 'If you are the Son of God' is highly misleading in this sense. It sounds as though the devil is taunting Jesus, questioning whether he really is the Son of God. In the Greek, however, the introductory word *ei* (translated by NIV as 'if') should really be rendered 'since'. The devil says to Jesus, 'Since you are the Son of God, tell these stones to become bread.' As most of the best commentaries therefore emphasize, Jesus' position as the Son of God is presupposed, not questioned.

Jesus, of course, had the *dunamis* or 'power' to perform the miracle suggested by Satan. There before his very eyes were flat, dry, desert stones which looked just like the kind of bread eaten in first-century Palestine. Jesus had the power to go up to those stones and to turn them into bread, in order to satisfy the raging hunger which we know he was experiencing at the time (he had, after all, fasted for forty days and forty nights). So why did he choose to say no? Why did he refuse the accuser?

The question needs asking because a few chapters later we see Jesus, the Spirit-filled Messiah, performing precisely such a miracle. Though in the following story bread is not created from stones, it is in a sense created and certainly created miraculously. We read in Matthew 14:15–21:

As evening approached, the disciples came to him and said, 'This is a remote place, and it's already getting late. Send the crowds away, so that they can go to the villages and buy themselves some food.'

Jesus replied, 'They do not need to go away. You give them something to eat.'

'We have here only five loaves of bread and two fish,' they answered.

'Bring them here to me,' he said. And he directed the people to sit down on the grass. Taking the five loaves and the two fish and looking up to heaven, he gave thanks and broke the loaves. Then he gave them to the disciples, and the disciples gave them to the people. They all ate and were satisfied, and the disciples picked up twelve basketfuls of broken pieces that were left over. The number of those who ate was about five thousand, besides women and children.

Reading this story after the temptation narrative, one has to ask why it is that Jesus will agree to create bread in Matthew 14, whilst he refuses to perform a very similar miracle in Matthew 4. Why is it permissible on the mountain but not in the desert? This question nags us even more because of Matthew's version of the saying concerning the request to fathers by their sons. Luke has the following saying:

Which of you fathers, if your son asks for a fish, will give him a snake instead? Or if he asks for an egg, will give him a scorpion? If you then, though you are evil, know how to give good gifts to your children, how much more will your Father in heaven give the Holy Spirit to those who ask him! (Luke 11:11–13).

Matthew's version of the same saying goes as follows:

Which of you, if his son asks for bread, will give him a stone? Or if he asks for a fish, will give him a snake? If you, then, though you are evil, know how to give good gifts to your

children, how much more will your Father in heaven give good
gifts to those who ask him! (Matthew 7:9–11).

The main difference between these two sayings is that God the
Father promises the Holy Spirit in Luke, whilst he promises
'good gifts' in Matthew. But there is another difference. In Luke
the earthly father is asked for a fish and an egg. In Matthew he
is asked for some bread and some fish. The mention of bread
and fish in Matthew's version of the saying links it straight away
with another story in which bread and fish are mentioned:
namely, the feeding of the five thousand, a story which is in
turn linked with the temptations of Jesus. The implication of
these subtle echo-effects is that we, the readers, know that our
Father in heaven is one who gives bread – not stones – when
asked. Going back to Matthew 4:1–11, where Jesus is tempted
to turn stones into bread, we are left asking, 'Why doesn't
Jesus ask God to do the very thing mentioned in Matthew 7:11
– especially if God is that kind of Father?'

The answer lies in this important concept of egoism – the
doctrine of self-interest. In Matthew 14, Jesus creates bread
using the spiritual gift of miraculous works because that bread
is required by others. The crowds, in short, are hungry. In
Matthew 4, however, Jesus has the choice of using the same
spiritual gift purely and exclusively for his own benefit – in
other words, to feed himself. In the first instance, the motive is
altruistic. In the second instance, it is egoistical. What Jesus is
refusing here is the temptation to use spiritual power for his
own comfort, blessing and benefit. He is refusing the temptation of charismatic egoism.

One of the major temptations in Pentecostal and Charismatic
circles has been precisely this: the temptation to confine demonstrations of the Spirit's power to the meeting place, when the
Lord wants signs and wonders in the marketplace as well. One of
the major items on the Lord's agenda right now is to remind
such churches that this power is, as the Classical Pentecostals
saw so clearly, 'power for service and mission', not power for
self-interest and self-indulgence. Paul clearly taught – by both

information and demonstration – that manifestations of the Spirit's power were to occur during the preaching of the Cross to the unconverted, not just in worship services for the converted:

> When I came to you, brothers, I did not come with eloquence or superior wisdom as I proclaimed to you the testimony about God. For I resolved to know nothing while I was with you except Jesus Christ and him crucified. I came to you in weakness and fear, and with much trembling. My message and my preaching were not with wise and persuasive words, but with a demonstration of the Spirit's power, so that your faith might not rest on men's wisdom, but on God's power. (1 Corinthians 2:1–5)

When Paul first carried the Gospel to Corinth, he entered the city and employed a strategy in which Word and Spirit, Scripture and Power, were wedded together. He preached the Gospel of the Cross to the unconverted – no doubt in the marketplaces as well as in the synagogues – and that message was accompanied by demonstrations of the power of the Holy Spirit – in conversions, healings, deliverance and other miracles. This same combination is stressed in Hebrews 2:3–4.

> This salvation, which was first announced by the Lord, was confirmed to us by those who heard him. God also testified to it by signs, wonders and various miracles, and gifts of the Holy Spirit distributed according to his will.

The same marriage of Gospel and gifts, of proclamation and power, is also stressed on just about every page of the Book of Acts. Indeed, Jesus promises that the power of the Holy Spirit will be given in order that the disciples can boldly declare the Good News:

> You will receive power when the Holy Spirit comes on you; and you will be my witnesses in Jerusalem, and in all Judea and Samaria, and to the ends of the earth (Acts 1:8).

The power of the Holy Spirit is therefore given in order that the Gospel should be declared with courage and conviction:

> After they prayed, the place where they were meeting was shaken. And they were all filled with the Holy Spirit and spoke the word of God boldly (Acts 4:31).

There is no doubt that this emphasis has been by and large lost in some contemporary Pentecostal and Charismatic churches. Demonstrations of the Spirit's power have been confined to worship services for the converted. They have not been occurring in the high streets and the pubs. Why? Because many of us as church leaders have forgotten the call to do the work of an evangelist and have therefore limited manifestations of the Holy Spirit to times of worship. We have, in effect, kept the power to ourselves and turned the gifts, at our worst, into part of a kind of in-house, supernatural entertainment. We have, in short, fallen for the temptation of charismatic egoism – of spiritual power for self-interest and self-indulgence.

It is my suspicion that the Lord is addressing this tendency in Pentecostal and Charismatic churches right now. Many of us have been guilty of selfishness in the Charismatic constituency. This – as always with selfishness – is sin, and the Lord has been causing many of us to repent of it by taking us through a desert experience. That desert experience has for many been a period in which the power of the Spirit has felt less present and when the gifts of the Spirit have seemed less visible and authentic. It has been an essential preparation for personal revival. During the year of 1994, however, the Lord has graciously provided a new outpouring of his Spirit. Innumerable Christians who were panting like the deer at the waterbrook have now been filled again. We who have been touched in such a profound way need to be careful not to fall again for the temptation of *charismatic egoism*. Having addressed this issue in the heat of the desert, we must be careful not to indulge in it again in a time of great blessing.

The Second Temptation
• •

If the first temptation was about charismatic egoism, the second consisted of what I call *charismatic exhibitionism*. Again, Matthew takes up the story:

> Then the devil took him to the holy city and had him stand on the highest point of the temple. 'If you are the Son of God,' he said, 'throw yourself down. For it is written: "He will command his angels concerning you, and they will lift you up in their hands, so that you will not strike your foot against a stone." '
>
> Jesus answered him, 'It is also written: "Do not put the Lord your God to the test." '

In this second temptation, the devil takes Jesus to the highest point of the temple building. That alone is significant symbolism. It symbolizes the loftiest heights of position, status and power. Indeed, we should remember that in Jewish thought Jerusalem was considered to be the centre of the world and the temple to be the highest point on the face of the earth. There, on the loftiest pinnacle, Jesus is urged by the devil to succumb to the temptation of performance. 'Make a spectacle,' he urges. 'Hurl yourself off the temple. Let the people see a great miracle as the angels catch you before you hit the ground!'

This, then, is the temptation to charismatic exhibitionism *par excellence*. My dictionary defines exhibitionism as 'extravagant behaviour aimed at drawing attention to oneself'. Defined in those terms we have to acknowledge once again that there has been a good deal of 'falling' in the area of this particular temptation, especially in Pentecostal and Charismatic circles. Many of us have fallen foul of what I call the platform disease – a disease in which we strive earnestly for a platform, and then seek to keep that platform through posturing behaviour and sensationalist talk. I have personally been guilty of this many times. Some of the pastors I have interviewed in preparation for this book – pastors who have been greatly blessed by the work of the Spirit in Toronto – have confessed the same thing to me. There is evidence everywhere of precisely this kind of vanity.

For example, not long ago a poster was put through my letter box inviting me to a healing meeting in a local Pentecostal church here in Sheffield. When I read the words on the poster I could hardly believe my eyes:

BRITAIN'S TOP HEALING MINISTRY

read the headline. Underneath,

Amazing healings of arthritis, depression, fears, blood disorders, Parkinson's disease, scores of other diseases . . . Sticks and crutches often discarded in Rev. X's meetings. Lives have been changed by the power of God. The blind have seen . . . The deaf have heard . . . The lame and crippled have walked after prayers in these services . . .

Other headlines grabbed my attention:

INCURABLE PEOPLE GET CURED!
Thousands of sick people flock to his services!
Everyone gets personal attention!

Then, on the other side, the words: 'One of the most successful and powerful gifts of healing in the world today!'

This kind of thing does not glorify God. It glorifies the minister. In fact, it is perhaps the most flagrant example of charismatic exhibitionism I have seen in recent years. The poster is littered with photographs of people dancing and leaping as if to underline rather than avoid the pitfalls of exhibitionism. You may think this is the exception, but it is in fact the tip of a very large and barely submerged iceberg in the fast-growing, Pentecostal and Charismatic sub-cultures. The temptation to Christian superstardom is no longer just confined to North American tele-evangelists. However, the Lord is disciplining his Church over this tendency. He shares his glory with no other.

Many leaders have found themselves led into a desert experience in which this vanity has had to be confronted head on. Many of us have had to deal with the pride and the vanity which has taken us up to the high pinnacles of the temple, where we have succumbed to the very temptation which our Lord so boldly resisted: sensationalist exhibitionism.

One person who has been taken through this process already is Rev. Sue Hope, vicar of Brightside and Wincobank (a deprived, urban priority area in Sheffield), member of general synod, and a leading figure in Anglicans for Renewal Ministries. Sue was very prominent in the press and on TV during the debate at general synod concerning the ordination of women to the priesthood. That gave her a public, national platform which – she confided – did her no good at all. Invitations and offers started to flood in. But all this flattery began to take its toll, and before long she was drained and disillusioned:

> I had grown very weary in ministry over the years, and although I had been committed to charismatic renewal, I had also become 'hardened' to the Holy Spirit. Ambition, vanity, self-seeking, were all operating covertly in my life.

God began to deal with this by taking Sue into the desert:

> 1994 began with the sudden death of my father, followed swiftly by two other enormously significant events – my ordination to the priesthood and a seven week sabbatical in Israel. I came back from Israel with some clear goals and priorities, about turning my back on self-seeking, about living as a person of the Beatitudes, about doing the works of Jesus rather than being on lots of committees!

At this point of repentance, of *metanoia* or 'about-turning', Sue heard about Toronto.

It was after I came back from Israel that I began to hear stories about Toronto, and I felt a curious 'quickening' inside as I listened and as I read. I have for many years been a cautious admirer of John Wimber and his ministry and have been blessed by his visits to this country, but I had never felt that I wanted to be wholly identified with him. With the benefit of hindsight I can see that this was because I was actually afraid of a close identification with this ministry, perhaps because I felt it would make me vulnerable to the kind of ridicule and rejection which is often suffered by those who dare to take Jesus at his word. So it was unusual that I felt stirred by what I was hearing about Toronto.

Sue felt compelled by the Holy Spirit to travel to Toronto, and her visit there turned out to be a real Damascus Road experience. In fact, it was for Sue as life-changing as her conversion to Christ twenty years ago. She writes:

I was filled deeply and wonderfully with the Holy Spirit, in a quite new and different manner. Times of resting in the Spirit were accompanied by a sense of the reality of God and of his presence, of words spoken to me in great love, of 'other realities' beyond this present world. Any fear that I had that this was just another Western 'feel-good' experience were swept away by my own experience of my creatureliness and smallness before a God who is totally 'other'. I found particularly moving the testimonies of pastors from the Third World, who were being profoundly healed and strengthened before returning to places of great suffering.

The effects of this powerful experience on Sue have been dramatic. No longer is she after a platform in the Anglican Church. She is after the way of the Spirit in her parish in Sheffield – an urban priority area at that. Sue's own words capture the fruit of her experience beautifully:

Since then I have become ignited with a fresh passion for the things of Christ, a deep hunger for his Word, a hunger for prayer (even to rising in the middle of the night *wanting* to pray!), a fresh delight in talking about Christ to those outside the church, a new confidence in my ministry. We have seen repentance among church members, deep healing from past wounds, a similar hunger for God, a true refreshing of our corporate life. We are now in the middle of a period of happy and holy chaos – by which I mean nothing is as well organized – but the church is enormously, indeed outrageously, happy, and we are taken up with loving the Lord. I am so grateful to him for what he has done for me, and for what he is doing for us all, for truly 'this is the Lord's doing, and it is wondrous in our eyes'.

Sue's story is a testimony of what happens when a person confesses that she has fallen for the sins of vanity and pride, and renounces the desire for a platform. The recent story of Eric Delve (formerly an itinerant evangelist) also illustrates this truth very powerfully. Part of Eric's testimony is included at the end of this chapter for discussion.

The Third Temptation

There is a third temptation in the story of Jesus' desert trek. This I describe as the temptation of *charismatic escapism*. Matthew continues the tale as follows:

> Again the devil took him to a very high mountain and showed him all the kingdoms of the world and their splendour. 'All this I will give you,' he said, 'if you will bow down and worship me.'
> Jesus said to him, 'Away from me, Satan! For it is written: "Worship the Lord your God, and serve him only." '

What was Satan offering Jesus here? He was offering Jesus something that was going to belong to him anyway. Once Jesus had completed the work his Father had given him to do, once he had paid the price of sin by dying on the Cross, God would highly exalt him and give him all authority in heaven and on earth (Matthew 28:18–20). When that occurred, Jesus would have all those things which the devil is promising here: 'all the kingdoms of the world and their splendour'. At the time of the temptations, these things belonged to Satan, who is described as the prince of this world. But by the time Jesus is crucified and risen, they will have been snatched from Satan and handed over to the Lord Jesus Christ, the King of kings. So what is Satan offering in the temptation story? He is offering Jesus the glory without the suffering, the prestige without the pain, the honour without the sacrifice. He is offering Jesus 'all the kingdoms of the world and their splendour', but without having to suffer the agony of the crucifixion.

This is the temptation of charismatic escapism. Satan is encouraging Jesus to avoid the grim ordeal of Calvary and head for glory without any hardship. Is there any of this kind of charismatic escapism in the renewed churches today? The answer to that has to be yes. I define escapism as the 'desire to escape from reality, particularly unpleasant or painful realities'. Put that way we can see that there is much of this in Pentecostal and Charismatic churches, as Tom Smail has recently pointed out. In a brilliant essay in the book *Charismatic Renewal: The Search for a Theology*, Smail goes back to Reformation theology in order to set the scene:

Martin Luther used to contrast what he called *theologia crucis*, the theology of the cross that was centred on the crucified Jesus, with *theologia gloriae*, the theology of glory that tried to deal with God in a way that did not take the cross fully into account. He knew very well that our sinful hearts are forever devising ways of evading the cross, because it is there that we are most radically judged in order that we may be most radically forgiven, and most deeply humbled in order that we may be most highly exalted.

Smail's point is that Pentecostal and Charismatic spirituality, generally speaking, derives from a theology of glory not a theology of the cross. In fact, Smail accuses Pentecostals of a glib triumphalism which has no room for unrelieved suffering and unanswered prayer. Confronted with these things, Pentecostals and Charismatics have no theology to guide them. In terms of Philippians 3:10, they have a spirituality in which they know Christ and the power of his resurrection, but they have not yet learned to share in the fellowship of his sufferings, becoming like him in his death.

Many Pentecostals who are facing persecution in Third-World contexts (such as, for example, Peru) will no doubt take exception to this, and rightly so. As we saw in chapter 1, Pentecostals are amongst the most harassed of all Christians in the world today. However, in more affluent and comfortable cultures – such as North America and Great Britain – Smail's critique is far more relevant and accurate. Pentecostals and Charismatics in these contexts have, at times, bought into a highly escapist theology, and this is particularly evident in those who have accepted the teachings of the so-called Faith Movement. This movement advocates the power of positive, verbal confession. In other words, it teaches a 'name it and claim it' philosophy in which I, the believer, claim the health and wealth which is rightfully mine in Christ. As Gloria Copeland has very recently put it:

> Everything we could ever need is waiting for us in the realm of the spirit with our name on it. All we need to do is get it from there to here. How do we do that? With faith. Faith is the 'currency' we use to transfer God's provision for us from the unseen realm of the spirit to this natural, earthly realm ... If you have an abundance of faith in your spiritual account, you can enjoy plenty of *everything* – wealth, health, good relationships, peace, success – because the Bible says God 'giveth us richly all things to enjoy'.
> (I Timothy 6:17).

This kind of prosperity Gospel proposes health and wealth as a fundamental right for every Christian, provided they have sufficient faith. Thus, when people become ill or have an accident, the idea is to believe and confess the Word. As you accept and declare God's Word in a situation, everything – from snake bites to cancer – will be supernaturally healed. Of course, the problem with all of this is that those who are not healed feel extremely guilty. They are told that they remain unhealed because they have insufficient faith. It is their fault. But is this really Biblical? The truth of the matter is that it is only partly Biblical. There is no doubt that God desires the best for us, and there is no doubt that words of faith have power. It is worth noting in this respect that Satan urges Jesus to '*tell* these stones to become bread'. He does not say '*turn* these stones into bread'. Even Satan, therefore, acknowledges the power of words spoken in faith. However, there is also little doubt that the Lord expects us to take up our cross daily and to live a life of costly discipleship. Ours is therefore an *austerity* not a *prosperity* Gospel. Any theology which leaves the dimension of suffering out of the picture is, in the final analysis, guilty of escapism.

Charismatic escapism is one of the things which the Lord wants us to renounce in the desert. He wants us to realize how cultural such escapist theologies are. Our culture, as I wrote in chapter 3, is an addictive, ecstatic culture. It is a culture in which literally hundreds of ways of removing pain are on offer to each one of us every day. Ingestive addictions (like Ecstasy), process addictions (like accumulating money), people addictions (such as sex), ideological addictions (like consumerism) and technological addictions (like computer games) are everywhere available, and all of them offer a temporary anaesthesia in which we can have our pain removed. But a state of permanent happiness is not our natural, human condition. A state of unrelieved euphoria is not how we are supposed to live. That is a cultural view, not a Biblical or a Christian view. Eternal ecstasy is for the not yet, not the now of the Kingdom of heaven. In the meantime there is often more agony (as in the New Testament word *agon*, struggle) than ecstasy. Suffering is a part of the normal charismatic life.

Later on in the gospel of Matthew this point is underlined at Caesarea Philippi. Peter confesses Jesus as the Messiah in Matthew 16:13–20, and Jesus applauds him for his confession. In the very next stage of the discussion, however, Jesus starts to spell out what kind of Messiah he is – one who will go to Jerusalem, suffer many things, and be killed. At this point Peter reacts sternly with the words, 'Never, Lord' – words that are potently and blatantly contradictory (for how can you say 'never' to the one you call 'Lord'?). Jesus then rebukes Peter with the words, 'Get behind me, Satan!' Satan is mentioned here because Peter is tempting Jesus in precisely the way we find in the temptation story in Matthew 4:1–11. He is encouraging Jesus to be a Messiah who bypasses suffering. So Jesus tells Peter what being a follower of the Way is really all about:

> If anyone would come after me, he must deny himself and take up his cross and follow me. For whoever wants to save his life will lose it, but whoever loses his life for me will find it.

What greater rebuke to charismatic escapism could there be than those words?

The Power of God's Word

My argument in this final chapter has been a simple one: the most essential preparation for personal revival in these days is the desert experience. This desert experience has, for many Pentecostals and Charismatics, been a time of testing in which the normal supports of life and ministry (particularly the manifest power of the Holy Spirit) have been withdrawn so that they can stand alone before the Living God to repent of certain worldly tendencies. These tendencies – which I have seen so often in myself – I have described as charismatic egoism (the desire to keep supernatural blessing for ourselves), charismatic exhibitionism (the desire for a platform and for sensationalist meetings) and charismatic escapism (the desire for a *theologia gloriae* rather than a *theologia crucis*). Dealing with that has indeed felt like discipline rather than delight, refining rather than refreshment.

What is it that sustains and refreshes us on our desert trek of repentance? If we go back to Matthew 4:1–11 it is clear that the thing that sustained the Lord Jesus was the Word of God. It was his profound knowledge of the Scriptures (particularly Deuteronomy 6–8) which enabled him to overcome the temptations of the one called 'the tempter' (*peirazon* in Matthew 4:3) and 'the devil' (*diabolos*, in Matthew 4:5,8,11). In his desert warfare with the enemy, it was the power of the sword of the Spirit, the Word of God (Ephesians 6:17) which defeated the onslaughts of the tempter. Jesus' ability to recall and to apply the Word of God with understanding and with power was what sustained, protected and empowered him in the desert.

Now that again is significant, particularly for Charismatics. Charismatic Christians in the 1980s were often guilty of having a spirituality of Spirit divorced from the Word, of power divorced from doctrine. At the turn of the present decade, this imbalance became a popular subject for many in the church, with books like *The Fourth Wave* (David Pawson), new partnerships (such as the one at Westminster Chapel between the evangelical R. T. Kendall and the charismatic Paul Cain), and teaching conferences (such as the Beulah conference on 'Word and Spirit' at Wembley) emerging. In the recent time of refining and refreshing, many of us who have been guilty of relying too much on subjective revelation have been drawn back to the Word of God. A new hunger for the Scriptures – particularly for discovering and understanding Scriptures which have a THIS-IS-THAT dynamic – has become evident amongst those affected by the Toronto blessing.

When we enter the desert experience, it is therefore the power and the beauty of God's Word which sustains, protects and empowers us. As the Accuser starts to do his malevolent work, we refuse him with the truths of Scripture. As the Adversary of the Most High God seeks to disrupt, deceive and destroy the elect, the elect in turn pierce him with the sword of the Spirit that is God's Word.

Crocuses in the Desert

One Scripture which is proving to be deeply beneficial to those who are in the desert is Isaiah 35. This magnificent passage gives us the Scriptural promises which enable us to refuse the Accuser in the desert. As we lay hold of these promises, and as we believe them in faith, the power of the enemy will diminish and the season of repentance will draw to a close. Isaiah prophesied:

> The desert and the parched land will be glad;
> the wilderness will rejoice and blossom.
> Like the crocus, it will burst into bloom;
> it will rejoice greatly and shout for joy.
> The glory of Lebanon will be given to it,
> the splendour of Carmel and Sharon;
> They will see the glory of the Lord,
> the splendour of our God.
> Strengthen the feeble hands,
> steady the knees that give way.
> Say to those with fearful hearts,
> 'Be strong, do not fear;
> Your God will come,
> he will come with vengeance;
> With divine retribution,
> he will come to save you.'

Then will the eyes of the blind be opened
  and the ears of the deaf unstopped.
Then will the lame leap like a deer,
  and the mute tongue shout for joy.
Water will gush forth in the wilderness
  and streams in the desert.
The burning sand will become a pool,
  the thirsty ground bubbling springs.
In the haunts where jackals once lay,
  grass and reeds and papyrus will grow.

And a highway will be there;
  it will be called the Way of Holiness.
The unclean will not journey on it;
  it will be for those who walk on that Way;
  wicked fools will not go about on it.
No lion will be there,
  nor will any ferocious beast get up on it;
  they will not be found there.
But only the redeemed will walk there,
  and the ransomed of the Lord will return.
They will enter Zion with singing;
  everlasting joy will crown their heads.
Gladness and joy will overtake them,
  and sorrow and sighing will flee away.

In the desert place, promises like these are truly nourishing
and vivifying. For those who know the dereliction, the
despair and the dryness of the desert experience, such words
can literally save lives. They are like crocuses in the desert.
This beautiful poetic image of the crocus is particularly relevant and poignant to me. When I was in the heart and the
heat of my own desert trek, I spoke honestly about my difficulties at a conference. A few weeks later, a very dear man of
God who had been at that conference wrote these words in
a letter to me:

I was very interested to hear you speak of your desert trek (spiritually) and the problems you are experiencing in parish ministry. Almost three years ago I had a sabbatical in Israel. Everyone was talking about the need for rain. There had not been any real 'winters' for four years. I walked along Wadi Qelt from Jerusalem to Jericho. To my horror I almost walked on a single crocus-like flower. Everywhere was barren except for this lovely flower. I stood and looked at it for a long time.

The rain and snow fell in Israel during the winter of 91/92 such as had not been experienced for 60 years. I met someone who was near Wadi Qelt in the spring of 1992 who told me she saw a miracle – millions of crocus-like flowers in the desert, the seeds having been buried for more than half a century. She reports that it was a wonderful sight.

What a beautiful picture of revival – of new life in the desert of repentance. That, friends, is what lies ahead of us. But first there is a season of refining to endure – a season ordained by the Lord. Just as Jesus was led into the desert by the Spirit, so are we. Just as for Jesus the desert experience was only for a season, so it is for us. If we can strengthen our feeble hands, steady the knees that give way, if we can encourage one another to be strong and to be hopeful, if we can allow the Lord to build his Highway of Holiness out of our tears of repentance – then we will see the eyes of the blind being opened, the ears of the deaf unstopped, the lame leaping like deer, and the tongues of the mute released to praise the Lord. Then we will see water in the desert, and green shoots in the burning sand. Then the season of singing will return, as the ransomed of the Lord go back to Zion with mouths full of laughter, with gladness and with shouts of joy. The time of sorrow and sighing will flee away on that day, and we will see the glory and the splendour of our God. As the letter-writer says,

God gives us a crocus in the desert (look for it!) as a sign of wonderful things to come. Years of faithful ministry produce a glorious sight to behold. This is the Lord's doing and it is marvellous in our eyes.

FOR FURTHER STUDY

Read the following extract from an article by Rev. Eric Delve, first published in *Anglicans For Renewal* magazine and reprinted with the kind permission of the editor, Rev. Michael Mitton. In this extract, Eric describes what turned out to be a painful 'desert experience'.

1 Which of the three temptations are relevant here – egoism, exhibitionism, escapism?

2 Which one had Eric fallen for?

3 What are the most noticeable things about this desert experience?

4 How would you have reacted in this situation?

5 Would you have been as honest as Eric?

6 Where has Eric found the beginnings of renewal?

In February 1993, Eric Delve was instituted as Vicar of St Lawrence's Church, Kirkdale (a UPA parish in Liverpool). He reflects here on the adjustment from travelling evangelist to parish priest.

The shift from a travelling ministry to a parochial one was the result and the cause of a revolution in my life. But I was reluctant to face the inevitable inner consequences. So it happened that I became embarrassingly aware of the changes that God was bringing about in me, at the very moment I was attempting to deny that any such change had occurred.

Asked to speak at the final evening meeting of *By My Spirit*, I found myself paralysed by sheer naked fear. Expectations were high. The other speakers had been excellent. Many of the people I love and respect most were there. It now remained for me to add the crowning address. I sensed that God was trying to say something to me. But I was too busy talking, to people. 'Networking' was my justification. In reality I had entered the second stage of fear where panic takes over.

Unable to receive what God was saying, I reverted to the past. It was not a case of David in Saul's armour, but Eric in Eric's old armour. Called upon to be vulnerable, I scuttled around like a hermit crab out of his shell, desperately picking up and pinning on pieces of protection from the past. Eventually covered with a hotchpotch of ideas and stories I emerged to take my place on the platform. When I had played my (overlong) part I sat down and heard God's voice clearly, saying 'I never want you to preach like that again.'

Looking back, the most painful moment for me was the point, familiar to most preachers, at which, knowing that I was thrashing about in a vain attempt to discover some spiritual life up there, I tried some self-justification. 'I am just a simple storyteller,' I disclaimed. Even as I said it I knew it was a lie. I was trying to justify my failure to listen to God by denying that he had asked me simply to speak his word. I had failed him.

Some people were touched. It made no difference. I knew I had faltered. I had refused to move on in ministry. It was the most humiliating failure of all my years in platform ministry: and therefore the most valuable. Something died in me that night. I hope it never rises again.

Looking back, I now feel that in my twenty years of life as a travelling evangelist, I collaborated with processes that tended to isolate me. In spite of my best efforts, I was increasingly cut off even from the very message I was preaching. I became drained, empty. I was not only scraping the barrel, I was digging holes through it. Using spiritual resources I did not possess, I was overdrawing, promising to pay back at some future date. I felt bankrupt. I arrived in the parish, delighted to be able to get off the treadmill, to be able to stand still. As part of this little Christian community, I have been able to draw from its treasures and on the resources of Scripture in a new way. Above all I have started to meet God again.

It is almost as if, in all my frantic activity, I was running so fast that I had outstripped the Spirit of God. Here, in a local ministry, focused on this area, I am learning to be still inside. Now the outer edges of the cloud of the Presence are beginning to touch me again. A tiny thrill of life shivers through me as I realize the truth – this place which I first thought was a wasteland is, in fact, an oasis. The parched land of my life is showing signs of regeneration – a tiny spring of fresh water is pressing up through the dry stones, the trickling is becoming a stream. I will try to remain in stillness. The fullness of the river cannot be far behind.

Conclusion:
The Unforgivable Sin

Looking over this book as a whole, I have argued that in Ezekiel 47:1–12 the writer depicts a fourfold pattern for spiritual renewal. I have also argued that this picture provides us with a framework for a historical overview of the work of God's Holy Spirit in the twentieth century. Clearly, the crucial thing to note from this is my belief that a fourth wave of the Holy Spirit is coming. The gaps between each wave have been getting progressively shorter. Between the first and the second wave (in terms of beginnings) there was about fifty years. Between the second and third there was about twenty years. If the Toronto blessing is the 'sea fret' of a fourth wave, the gap in time between the third and fourth wave will be only about ten years. Observing the growing impetus and momentum of the Spirit's work throughout the century – as well as the present socio-economic conditions of our society, and the poverty of the churches right now – I have to say that the time feels right.

But that still leaves us with the question, 'What is the Toronto blessing?' The first thing to say is that it is not yet a revival in the strictest sense. Our analysis of revivals in chapter 2 made this point. Whilst the Toronto blessing has many of the characteristics of revival, it has not yet developed that evangelistic, centrifugal emphasis which was so visible in the birth of Pentecostalism and in the astonishing events in Wales during 1904. Large numbers of converts are not yet being reported. The primary and most noticeable characteristic about the Toronto blessing has been the refreshing of weary pastors and the return of wandering prodigals. The emphasis, in other words, has been on 'restoration' – restoring the first love of battle-worn ministers and lapsed Christians. Not surprisingly, therefore, laughter and joy have been dominant features. As in many of the stories recorded in Luke 15, there is always a party when something or someone who is lost is subsequently restored.

Times of Refreshing

The best phrase to describe this movement of God is 'a time of refreshing from the Lord'. In Acts 3:19–20, Peter says to the men of Israel:

> Repent, then, and turn to God, so that your sins may be wiped out, that times of refreshing may come from the Lord, and that he may send the Christ, who has been appointed for you – even Jesus.

With this statement we enter again into the THIS-IS-THAT dynamic mentioned at the start of this book. Here again many leaders are proposing that the THIS which is occurring in Toronto and throughout the world is THAT articulated by Peter in Acts 3. This applies to every aspect of Acts 3:19–20, which may be divided as follows:

1 Repentance [of sins]

2 Refreshment [of believers]

3 Return [of Christ]

Thus, many of those caught up in the present work of the Spirit are finding themselves taken through times of repentance. My wife Alie spent two weeks weeping over her sins before her 'time of refreshing' came. I know of at least one other person in our church who has experienced something very similar. I believe that there will be a profound season of repentance for the whole church very soon.

But refreshment is also a common theme. Times of refreshing seems a very apt phrase here. In the original Greek the phrase is *kairoi anapsucheos*. The word *kairos* denotes a sovereignly ordained season, a unique period of time which is planned by God. We should note that the word is in the plural, *kairoi*, and that Peter is therefore speaking of more than one such season. *Anapsucheos* is the genitive singular of *anapsuchis*, a noun rarely used in the New Testament but which literally means 'a breathing space', 'a short time of relief and relaxation'. In a figurative sense this word is used by Peter in Acts 3:19 to refer to seasons of rest and renewal during the Messianic Age. This, many propose, is exactly what the Lord is giving us right now – a 'breather' before a huge advance of the Kingdom which will require great courage and commitment on our part.

Repentance and refreshment are therefore key themes of both the Toronto blessing and of Peter's words in Acts 3:19. But there is more. Many people have experienced a heightened sense of expectation concerning the Second Coming of our Lord Jesus Christ. One lady recently wrote to me,

> I believe God the Father is preparing his people by the power of the presence of the Holy Spirit for the second coming of our Lord and Saviour, our Redeemer and king – Christ Jesus! We must be awake – alert – ready to go, and also helping to prepare others.

This intensified sense of the reality and the significance of the *parousia* of Jesus has become one of the noticeable features of the present move of the Spirit. This nearly always occurs during times of renewal, as we observed in chapter 1. There I showed how eschatological fervour resulted from all three waves of the Spirit – classical Pentecostalism, Charismatic renewal and Protestant evangelical renewal. As to how soon that great day will be, no one of course knows except the Father. The most sensible thing to say is that it will be a lot nearer when you read these words than it is now as I write them.

Blaspheming Against the Spirit

If the Toronto blessing is the birthing of something so immensely significant for the world (as well as the Church), then two groups of people need to be very careful not to commit the unforgiveable sin – namely, blaspheming against the Holy Spirit. What, then, is blasphemy against the Holy Spirit? And who are the two groups of people who need to guard against it?

The phrase 'blasphemy against the Holy Spirit' occurs in the verb form in Mark 3:29, Matthew 12:32 and Luke 12:10. The saying is similar in all three versions:

MARK	MATTHEW	LUKE
I tell you the truth, all the sins and blasphemies of men will be forgiven them. But whoever blasphemes against the Holy Spirit will never be forgiven; he is guilty of an eternal sin.	Anyone who speaks a word against the Son of Man will be forgiven, but anyone who speaks against the Holy Spirit will not be forgiven, either in this age or in the age to come.	Everyone who speaks against the Son of Man will be forgiven, but anyone who blasphemes against the Holy Spirit will not be forgiven.

Both Mark and Matthew place this saying about blaspheming against the Holy Spirit in the context of a controversy with various religious groupings – the teachers of the law (Mark 3:22) and the Pharisees (Matthew 12:24). The issue is whether Jesus is performing extraordinary deeds by the power of the Holy Spirit or by the power of Satan. As far as Mark and Matthew are concerned, Jesus is the charismatic Messiah who operates with the power of the Holy Spirit, which is the power of the kingdom of God. As far as the Pharisees are concerned, however, Jesus' works are occult demonstrations. They are, in short, demonic. Jesus repudiates this claim by saying, 'How can Satan drive out Satan?' He then proceeds to issue a warning, a warning which can be paraphrased thus: 'Be very careful what you say. If you call the works of the Holy Spirit demonic in origin and character you are on very dangerous ground indeed. That is called "blaspheming against the Holy Spirit", and that is an unforgivable sin.'

For Mark and Matthew, therefore, blaspheming against the Holy Spirit means describing the works of the Spirit as evil. For Luke, however, the situation is altogether different. He places the saying about blasphemy against the Holy Spirit in a very different context. Instead of a controversy concerning the deliverance of a demon-possessed man, we now have a block of teaching on the important Lukan theme of witnessing:

> I tell you, whoever acknowledges me before men,
> the Son of Man will also acknowledge before the
> angels of God. But he who disowns me before men
> will be disowned before the angels of God.
> And everyone who speaks a word against the Son
> of Man will be forgiven, but anyone who blasphemes
> against the Holy Spirit will not be forgiven.
> When you are brought before synagogues, rulers
> and authorities, do not worry about how you will
> defend yourselves or what you will say, for the Holy
> Spirit will teach you at that time what you should say.

Notice how the immediately preceding text (Luke 12:8) is about publicly acknowledging Jesus before men (i.e. witnessing). Notice how the text immediately following it (Luke 12:11–12) is a saying about the power of the Holy Spirit enabling persecuted Christians to give inspired witness under trial. The context is therefore one concerning witnessing, not calling good things evil. If we set Luke's version alongside Mark's, the differences between Luke's understanding of the unforgivable sin and Mark's become plain:

MARK 3:20–30

Then Jesus entered a house, and again a crowd gathered, so that he and his disciples were not even able to eat. When his family heard about this, they went to take charge of him, for they said, 'He is out of his mind.' And the teachers of the law who came down from Jerusalem said, 'He is possessed by Beelzebub! By the prince of demons he is driving out demons!'

So Jesus called them and spoke to them in parables: 'How can Satan drive out Satan? If a kingdom is divided against itself, that kingdom cannot stand. If a house is divided against itself, that house cannot stand. And if Satan opposes himself and is divided, he cannot stand; his end has come. In fact, no one can enter a strong man's house and carry off his possessions unless he first ties up the strong man. Then he can rob his house. I tell you the truth, all the sins and blasphemies of men will be forgiven them. But whoever blasphemes against the Holy Spirit will never be forgiven; he is guilty of an eternal sin.'

LUKE 12:8–12

'I tell you, whoever acknowledges me before men, the Son of Man will acknowledge before the angels of God. But he who disowns me before men will be disowned before the angels of God. And everyone who speaks a word against the Son of Man will be forgiven, but anyone who blasphemes against the Holy Spirit will not be forgiven. When you are brought before synagogues, rulers and authorities, do not worry about how you will defend yourselves or what you will say, for the Holy Spirit will teach you at that time what you should say.'

He said this because they
were saying, 'He has an evil
spirit.'

Thus whilst Mark and Matthew understand 'blaspheming
against the Holy Spirit' to mean 'calling the works of the Holy
Spirit demonic', Luke understands the same sin as failing to
witness to others once we have been filled with the Holy Spirit.

Calling Good Things Evil

Returning to the second question, 'Who are the two groups in
our own day who need to be careful?' The first group consists
of those who are opposed to the Toronto blessing. There are a
number of people in the church who correspond to Mark's
'teachers of the law' and Matthew's 'Pharisees'. They are very
religious people. Some of them love the church (perhaps a little
more than they should). Some of them read the Word and are
wholeheartedly committed to Bible study and teaching. But in
spite of these dutiful qualities, they are hostile and resistant
when it comes to the current work of the Holy Spirit – which
is, of course, unusual, dynamic, experiential and highly disturbing. In many cases, these people are saying extremely
negative things about the things which God is doing. The
following extract from a letter sent to me several months ago
will have to suffice as just one example amongst many:

> . . . many consider the Toronto phenomenon is not a blessing
> but a deception of Satan allowed by God in judgment on the
> house of God (I Peter 4:17) that lusts for experience rather
> than God himself (Psalm 106: 14–15). Do you not recognize
> the way the proponents speak of 'it' and 'thing' and
> occasionally of 'the presence of God' (which can be
> counterfeited by Satan) and not of knowing God. The
> compulsion to pass it on is another mark of a work of Satan.
> There is also a clearly hypnotic element in it. And those who

support it and have received it often become very aggressive when challenged. Does that speak of a source that is Godly?

When I receive letters (or hear comments) like this my heart is greatly troubled. There is so much that is deceived here. For example, the notion that something like the Toronto blessing cannot be of God because the Holy Spirit is not passed on like this. That is quite clearly wrong. There is what I call a doctrine of charismatic succession in Scripture. Did not Moses pass on his anointing to seventy elders? Did not Elijah do the same with Elisha? Did not, in a sense, Jesus do this with his own followers? The answer to each of those questions is a re-sounding YES! Furthermore, if the experiential dimension of the Toronto blessing (i.e. the manifestations) is motivated by Satan, then how come these experiences are – in the vast majority of cases – leading to a greater intimacy with Jesus, a greater adoration of God, a greater desire to pray, a greater love for the Scriptures, a greater joy in believing, a greater sense of wholeness, a greater sense of the *parousia*, and so on? What on earth could Satan achieve through all that!?

It needs to be said here that those of a conservative evangeli-cal or of an institutional mind-set need to be very careful not to blaspheme against the Holy Spirit (in the sense understood by Mark and Matthew) when they speak about the Toronto blessing. A much more Godly response from the sceptics would be that of Gamaliel in Acts 5:38:

> Therefore, in the present case, I advise you: Leave these men alone! Let them go! For if their purpose or their activity is of human origin, it will fail. But if it is from God, you will not be able to stop these men; you will only find yourselves fighting against God.

If you are a sceptic, I respectfully counsel you to take this line.

Failing to Witness
• • • • • • • • • • • • • • • • • •

There is, however a second danger. This applies to the second
group mentioned earlier. This group comprises those who
have been blessed by the Toronto phenomenon and who have
received a new lease of spiritual life – those, in other words,
who have been to meetings and experienced God's Spirit in a
new way. Some members of this group are in particular danger
of misunderstanding the whole purpose of the blessing. I have
heard it said by a number of leaders that we are to get as much
of the blessing as possible, that we are to keep on going to
meetings to be filled, and that we are to receive as much as we
can while it is here. That is very dubious teaching. The fact of
the matter is this: Luke quite plainly demonstrates, in both his
gospel and its sequel, that the reason why we are filled with the
Holy Spirit is so that we can give inspired witness to the rich
truths of the Good News. The power of the Spirit is not given
for self-gratification but for mission (Acts 1:8). Failure to
recognize and teach this, along with a concomitant encouragement of selfish charismatic praxis, will lead us perilously close
to blaspheming against the Holy Spirit in the Lukan sense.
Those of us who have been blessed need therefore to be aware!

In the final analysis, we do need to understand that God will
not go on filling a full bucket for ever. Even a gracious, extravagant loving Father will eventually have to remind us that the
blessing is for the battle, that the power is for proclamation.
This came home to me very forcibly when I was on the staff at
St Thomas' Crookes, one of the leading charismatic churches
in Great Britain. When I was there I believe some of us were
guilty of power fellowship (Michael Mitton's phrase) when
the Lord was calling us to power evangelism (John Wimber's
phrase). During that time, a woman who operated in the gift of
prophecy stood up on the Saturday evening of a weekend of
teaching on 'Servant Evangelism'. Afterwards she wrote up her
vision in the following words:

> I was reminded of a picture from three years ago of Crookes

Main Road. It was flooded with water – waves and waves of water washing up – flowing up from Broomhill and onto Crookes and down to the Bus 52 terminus. It was pouring and pouring, wave after wave. This then started to flow down hill and up hill – down School Road, Springvale, up Duncan Road, Cross Lane, and to the houses on these roads. It was incessant and the thought came to me, 'I am giving you living water – you do not see the source, but I am the source.' But as I watched the picture was changed; there were lots of people coming out of St Thomas' and Wesley Hall onto the streets of Crookes and they were all carrying buckets on one arm, holding white plastic cups in the other hand. There were hundreds of people pouring out and up the road with buckets – some full to the brim and overflowing, some half empty and some with only a little water in the bottom of the bucket. We, the people, were moving along, giving drinks to all the houses and shops, from the buckets, whether empty or full, giving it away. There were people's hands reaching out from the shops, all the shops, the pubs, and houses, taking the drinks. The people said, 'We've been waiting for you to come. We're so thirsty.' The flow of people began to move up the side roads and down the hills, all carrying the buckets, giving and giving. I heard a voice saying, 'Don't be afraid to give away what you have. Give away the little and I will give you more. Give even a cup of cold water in my name. Don't be afraid to touch their hands, to meet their eyes, to see and to feel their pain. For you are the river; you are the flow. I have prepared the way in the past, sending waves of water to clean and wash and prepare these streets. This I have already done. You are the river now. Give away what you have, for the people are waiting!'

These words are a timely reminder to us that the Lord fills us in order that we may reach out to the world. He enables us to receive a blessing in order that we may be a blessing. He gives us gifts in order that we may give them away. Only if the churches affected by the Toronto blessing develop an outer-directed focus will this time of refreshing turn into a revival. Only if we are prepared to go into the unchurched communities where we live, in order to speak charismatically of the wonders of Calvary, will this work develop into something which truly affects the world.

The Next Step
• • • • • • • • • • • • • •

The unforgivable sin is therefore understood differently by Matthew and Mark, on the one hand, and by Luke on the other. All three agree that this sin is all to do with what we say. Matthew and Mark agree that blaspheming against the Holy Spirit consists of calling the works of the Holy Spirit evil. In Matthew's account, this leads on to some stern warnings about careless talk.

In Luke's understanding of the blasphemy against the Holy Spirit, the issue at stake is not so much what we say (about charismatic manifestations) but about what we do not say – in other words, it is about a failure to speak inspirationally of Jesus.

Whatever group we identify with, the next step seems to me to be prayer. There are major issues in the Church which require that we fall to our knees in repentant prayer. There is the careless talk about the Holy Spirit mentioned above. There is the failure to recognize our selfishness in the context of the charismatic. There is the poverty of the Church – its irrelevance and ineffectiveness in a nation dizzy with all kinds of addictions, a nation looking for spiritual fulfilment in so many places other than Jesus Christ. There is the compromise of the Church over issues of money, sex and power. All these things are matters for urgent repentant prayer. But this kind of prayer is not to last forever, otherwise we shall become guilty of a new form of self-absorption. Sooner or later the Father will want to turn this prayer outwards into potent intercession for the world. When that occurs, I believe in my heart that the thing which is in every true Christian's heart will start to become a reality – namely, REVIVAL – and revival will be when the river of blessing bursts out of the Temple courts, through the Temple gates, and out into the Arabah – the Great Depression – where's God's people have been absent for far too long.

Bibliography
of Works Consulted

Barrett, D., 'Global Statistics', in *Dictionary of Pentecostal and Charismatic Movements* (see under Burgess below) pp. 810–29.

Bartleman, F., *What Really Happened at Asuza Street?* Northridge, California: Voice Christian Publications Inc., 1962 (original edition, 1925).

Bennett, D., *Nine O'Clock in the Morning*, Eastbourne, E. Sussex, Kingsway, 1992 (copyright, Logos International, 1970).

Burgess, S. & McGee, G. (eds), *Dictionary of Pentecostal and Charismatic Movements*, Grand Rapids, Michigan, Zondervan, 1990 (4th printing).

Clinebell, H., 'Philosophical-Religious Factors in the Etiology and Treatment of Alcoholism', in *Quarterly Journal of Studies on Alcohol*, Vol. 24. 1963, pp. 473–88.

Davis, R. E., *I Will Pour out my Spirit: A History and Theology of Revivals and Evangelical Awakenings*, Tonbridge Wells, Kent, Monarch, 1992.

Hocken, P., *Streams of Renewal: The Origins and Early Development of the Charismatic Movement in Great Britain*, Exeter, Paternoster Press, 1986.
The Glory and the Shame: Reflections on the 20th Century Outpouring of the Holy Spirit, Guildford, Surrey, Eagle, 1994.

Jones, R. B., *Rent Heavens: The Revival of 1904*, London, Pioneer Mission, 1948 (2nd edition).

Kruschel, K. J., *Laughter: A Theological Reflection*, London, SCM Press, 1994 (trans. John Bowden).

Kydd, R., *Charismatic Gifts in the Early Church*, Peabody, MS, Hendrickson, 1984.

Land, S., *Pentecostal Spirituality: A Passion for the Kingdom*, Sheffield, Sheffield Academic Press, 1993.

Lecky, W., *A History of England in the Eighteenth Century*. Vol. 1., London, Longmans, Green & Co, 1883.

Lincoln, A. *Ephesians*, Word Biblical Commentary, Dallas, 1990.

Lindbeck, G., *The Nature of Doctrine, Religion and Theology in a Postliberal Age*, Philadelphia, Westminster Press, 1984.

MacNutt, F., *Overcome by the Spirit*, Guildford, Surrey, Eagle, 1994.

Moltmann, J., *Spirit of Life: A Universal Affirmation*, London, SCM Press, 1992 (trans. Margaret Kohl).
Theology and Joy, London & New York, 1973.

Porter, R. *English Society in the Eighteenth Century*, London, Penguin, 1993.

Rogers, C., 'The Dionysian Background of Ephesians 5:18', *BibSac.* Vol. 136, 1979, pp. 249–57.

Shelton, J., *Mighty in Word and Deed: The Role of the Holy Spirit in Luke – Acts*, Peabody, MS, Hendrickson, 1991.

Smail, T., 'The Cross and the Spirit: Towards a Theology of Renewal', in Smail, T., Walker, A. & Wright, N., *Charismatic Renewal: The Search for a Theology*, London, SPCK, 1993, pp. 49–70.

Stibbe, M. W. G., 'The Theology of Renewal and the Renewal of Theology', *Journal of Pentecostal Theology* Vol. 3, 1993, pp. 71–90.
O Brave New Church: Rescuing An Addictive Culture, London, Darton Longman & Todd, 1995.

Suurmond, J. J., *Word and Spirit at Play: Towards a Charismatic Theology*, London, SCM, 1994 (Trans. John Bowden).

Taylor, J. *Ezekiel*, Tyndale Commentaries, Leicester, IVP, 1969.

Wagner, P., 'The Third Wave', in *Dictionary of Pentecostal and Charismatic Movements* (see under Burgess above), pp. 843–4.

Index
of Authors and Subjects